D0398592

CAGE RAT

CAGE RAT

LESSONS FROM A LIFE IN BASEBALL
BY THE YANKEES HITTING COACH

KEVIN LONG

WITH GLEN WAGGONER

ecco

An Imprint of HarperCollinsPublishers

HarperCollins books may be purchased for educational, business, or sales promotional use. For information please write: Special Markets Department, HarperCollins Publishers, 10 East 53rd Street, New York, NY 10022.

FIRST EDITION

Library of Congress Cataloging-in-Publication Data has been applied for.

ISBN 978-0-06-199499-9

11 12 13 14 15   OV/RRD   10 9 8 7 6 5 4 3 2 1

To Marcey
Thanks, baby . . .
For being the most amazing wife a man could ask for . . .
For being my best friend, confidante, and lover for life . . .
For being the best mom in the world to our three kids . . .
For all your support and love, every step of our way together.
Thanks, baby!

To Britney, Tracy, and Jaron
You guys are almost as amazing as your mother.
Thanks for all your understanding and support.
We made it on nothing but love for a lot of years,
but you hung in there like champions.

ACKNOWLEDGMENTS

A lot of people, many of whom I met for the first time in the last eighteen months, deserve credit for helping make *Cage Rat* happen, but I want to start with what has always been my primary source of strength and inspiration: my family.

Thanks first to my parents, Donna and Gary, for teaching me right from wrong and for always being there for me. And then there's Tim, my kid brother. Your unconditional love is so heartfelt that it's hard to believe we actually used to fight like . . . well, like brothers just two years apart. Grandma Jane, you are a living wonder, still going at ninety-two. (Dear reader, if you've never had a Grandma Jane, then you've never had a woman who simply did it all.) Marcey and I couldn't have done without you guys.

My beautiful Marcey blessed me with a great extended family. Slim (that would be Dennis Peed, Marcey's dad), we miss you so much. Carolyn (Marcey's mom), you are a tremendous lady who continues to amaze me with your strength. Lisa, you are the loving sister I never had. Mike and David, a guy can always use an extra couple of fine brothers. Thanks for your support and jumping on the Yankees bandwagon.

Between us, Marcey and I have a big, wonderful collection of aunts and uncles, nieces and nephews, grandmas and grandpas. Hey, gang, I love you all!

U of A! U of A! A big shout-out to all my teammates at the University of Arizona who taught me how to grow up and paved the road to my success—especially Lance Dickson, Scott Erickson, Chip Hale, Frank Halkovich, Trevor Hoffman, Todd Ingram, Jason Klonoski, Damon Mashore, Gar Millay, J. T. Snow, and Alan Zinter. We were led by the greatest college coaching staff ever assembled: head coach Jerry Kindall, who probably prayed more for me than for any player he ever coached; Jerry Stitt, the best hitting coach I ever had; and Jim Wing, our pitching coach, the most thoughtful man a teenager could be around.

Three coaches made their mark on me before I went off to college: Larry Waters, who made me a first-round draft pick when I was just ten years old; Owen DeJanovich, my high school coach in my first love, football; and my father, Gary Long, who was always willing to play catch and throw BP to his son, even after working ten-hour days.

A special thanks to a huge part of my family today, the New York Yankees. I consider myself blessed to be a part of the greatest organization in sports history. Learning at the feet of Joe Torre and Joe Girardi? Talk about hitting the lottery! Marcey and I have a remarkable bond with the other coaches and their wives. Thanks to our front office staff and scouting team—what a great gang!—and, of course, to the Steinbrenner family, who make it all come together.

Brian Cashman, you hired an unknown and gave him a chance to work on the biggest stage in sports. Thanks, man! I told you I wouldn't let you down.

I tip my cap to all the players I have coached along the way. Trust me, guys, nothing has made me happier over the years than to watch you make yourselves into better hitters. You make me proud.

A whole slew of people helped me get my memories and ideas down on paper. Thanks for guiding me on this journey and for catching me when I stumbled. Writer Glen Waggoner is a confessed longtime Yankees hater; he likes some team called the "Glenwag Goners" in some outfit called "Rotisserie League Baseball." Whatever, he can be my translator anytime. My publisher at Ecco, Daniel Halpern, had to put up with Glen and me, and managed to keep this project afloat. He *is* a Yankees fan, and a knowledgeable one at that. Thanks, Dan—I have found a friend for life. Associate editor Libby Edelson did a ton of heavy lifting behind the scenes and saved me from a lot of E-KLs. Tom Hopke, of HarperCollins, is a true baseball fanatic. (And, yes, a Yankees fanatic.)

To Alex Rodriguez and Robinson Cano, please accept my sincere gratitude for the stories you tell about me in the introduction and afterword. Thanks, guys.

I owe a special debt to Ray Négron, a true Yankee if there ever was one, who had the initial vision for this book and kept pushing me to write it. I thank you from my heart, Ray.

Finally, my starting lineup: Marcey, Britney, Tracy, and Jaron. And our amazing son-in-law, Mark, and our grandson, Jackson. We made it, guys!

CONTENTS

THANKS, COACH

BY ALEX RODRIGUEZ

Kevin Long and I first met in Tampa in 2004 during spring training, but we didn't really start getting to know each other until that September. That's when major-league rosters expand from twenty-five to forty, and also when a few coaches move from the minors to the big club—Kevin came up from Columbus. We hit it off right out of the box, and we talked some about hitting, sure, but we didn't really work together. Don Mattingly was the Yankees' hitting coach, so even though Kevin and I wore the same uniform, our relationship at first was personal rather than professional. The next year, same deal—we talked some during spring training '05, and then that September he came up during roster expansion, plus we continued to talk during spring training in 2006. During those brief encounters, our relationship picked up a little momentum on its way to becoming a great friendship.

That early friendship turned out to be really important to me after the 2006 season, when I asked him for a huge favor.

I felt like I'd struggled during the 2006 season, and the day that Detroit knocked us out in the AL Division Series, I knew what I needed to do about it. I promised myself, Donnie, manager Joe Torre, and general manager Brian Cashman that I was going to go home to Florida and get into a really intense workout regimen for the winter, and get my game back to where I thought it should be. That is, I would spend the off-season trying to figure out what was broken and fix it.

Turned out that Kevin would play a big part in that. Early that fall, the Yankees promoted Donnie to bench coach and named Kevin hitting coach, so when he called up just to say hello, like he did with all the other guys, I jumped at the opportunity and asked him if he could possibly come see me in Florida so we could work on some things.

That was asking a lot. Kevin lives in Arizona, so it wasn't like I was offering him a vacation from the winter cold or anything. Plus he has a family that he adores. But he said "Yes, sure" in a New York minute. He came over to my home in Coral Gables, Florida, in early December, and we went right to work in my batting cage. (By the way, the title of this book? An absolutely *perfect* description of my good friend, Mr. Kevin Long.) We spent four days together that first trip, and he came back in mid-January for a quick visit to see how I was doing with the things we'd talked about and worked on. Since then, a winter workout together has become part of our off-season routine, no matter what kind of season I'm coming off of.

One big thing about Kevin—make that one *huge* thing—is that within five minutes after meeting him, I knew that this was the kind of guy I could trust. I sensed immediately—it came through loud and clear—that this guy wasn't going to bullshit me about anything. That's why Kevin and I were good from day one.

At first, though, I didn't know exactly what to expect. He was a really nice guy and all, but we'd never worked together on my swing. Once we started talking about our philosophies a little bit, I discovered Kevin reminded me of Rudy Jaramillo, whom I worked with when I was with the Rangers, and who I think is one of the greatest hitting coaches out there. Kevin was saying a lot of the same things that Rudy said to me, and it made me feel very comfortable right away.

When a guy is as knowledgeable about the game as Kevin is, when he has as much passion for it as Kevin has, when he has a work ethic that I think may be even greater than my own—well, we found our common ground.

"Kevin, you have a blank canvas. I'm not happy with where my game is. I'm all ears. I'm just gonna listen to you, because I really want to get my game back to where I think it should be. You tell me what to do, and I'll bust my butt trying to do it."

Those are pretty near my exact words to Kevin when we got together that first time. It helped, I think—at least in my mind—that we had a blank canvas to work on. I've always believed that it's much easier to go from bad to great than from good to great. Maybe that's crazy, but I wanted to start from scratch. And I think that Kevin liked the fact that he was able to come in and speak his mind with no hesitation. Hitting 101, that's what it was.

Beginning in our first season together, 2007, when I had the best year of my baseball career (at least so far!), we set a pattern of talking every day before, during, and often after a game. Some days a little, some days a lot. But we talked: there was never a shortage of communication between us. We've become so good at our back-and-forth that sometimes all it takes is just a look, a phrase, or a word for Kevin to get his message across. For instance, if I take a bad swing and I glance over at Kevin standing at the edge of the dugout, he might just mouth the word *foot*. I can't hear one word, but I can see it, and I know what he's saying: "Alex! Remember, when you pick your front foot up, put it down in the same place as you swing. Don't stride forward!"

I can't tell you how many times I've started a game with a lousy at bat, a really bad one, and Kevin will say just one little thing to me back in the dugout, and I end up with 2-for-4, a couple of homers, and 5 RBIs, and we win the game. One *little* thing is often all it takes, because a baseball swing is composed of a lot of little things, and if one of those is off, all you can do is go back and take a seat and hope the next guy gets a hit.

A hitting coach has to have great eyes: he must be able to recognize immediately what a guy is doing wrong at the plate. Once he's spotted something wrong—and usually he's the only guy in the ballpark who has—your hitting coach has to be able to convey it clearly, concisely, and constructively. The last bit is super important: he can't say, "Alex, you really sucked on that last swing." He has to say something positive like, "Alex, get your hands up just a tad next time. You're going to nail this guy." That way, I take a positive image of what I need to do right the next time I go to the plate, not a negative image of what I did wrong the previous at bat.

That's one area where I think Kevin and I are really tight. He has the eyes and understanding to spot a tiny flaw and communicate that finding constructively, and I have the ears and understanding to grasp what he's saying and the talent to put his advice to work. We make a good combo because we trust each other 100 percent.

"Different strokes for different folks." You've heard that a million times, so let me explain one of Kevin's special talents another way. If Kevin Long worked on cars rather than batting swings for a living, he'd be an equally great technician with three types of cars: Hondas, Mercedes-Benzes, and Ferraris. Not every teacher—and that's what a hitting coach is, a teacher—can do that. Too many, in fact, teach the same way across the board: "Different folks, *just one* stroke."

Kevin has thirteen *swings* to know inside out, but he's also got thirteen different *personalities* to know inside out. That's because so much of hitting is psychological that he has to be a therapist as well as a technician.

Understand, too, that it's a year-round deal for Kevin. For him, the season doesn't end with the last out in one year and begin with the first day of spring training in the next. I sometimes think he doesn't know the meaning of *off*-season. I know he's been available for me and my teammates even though the calendar says November, December, or January.

Remember, the man *is* a cage rat.

Mastering the baseball swing is the hardest thing to do in all of sports. That's why nobody has ever done it. Mastered it, that is. Not

Babe Ruth, Ted Williams, Willie Mays, George Brett, or Hank Aaron, not any other superstar you can name.

Master the baseball swing? Can't be done. If you have the talent, the right coaching, a strong work ethic, and a whole lot of luck, you can get better. But as Kevin will be the first to remind you, a guy who hits .400 is *still* failing to do his job 60 percent of the time. So if you want to get better, if you want to go from good to great, you can't let yourself get down if you go 0-for-4, or even 0-for-16. That's the really hard part of this game, accepting how hard it is to take a piece of wood about a yard long and make a decision in a fraction of a second whether to swing at a ball that's coming at you at, like, ninety-plus miles an hour—and then, if you do swing, hit it solid.

One of Kevin's greatest strengths, in my estimation, is that he's able to take a thing that's super complicated, the sports equivalent of advanced calculus, and simplify it into a very easy 2 + 2 = 4. That's a gift. Not everybody has that gift.

For sure not everybody has Kevin's work ethic. *Hard work!* Kevin will tell you that's the key to getting better, no matter what you're trying to do. And I think that message comes through loud and clear in this book.

My road to the big leagues was so much easier than Kevin's. I mean, I basically went from my senior prom to the majors. Kevin's journey was a little different: he went from the prom to eighteen years in the minor leagues and only then as a coach into the big leagues. I have a tremendous appreciation for what he's done. If you're a high school ballplayer and want to improve your hitting, this book is a must-read. Ditto if you're a longtime baseball fan who wants to get more inside the game. And if you're looking for a role model . . .

Kevin Long's life story is more than just a story about baseball. *Cage Rat* is a story about living the American dream. No, he didn't make the majors as a player; his first dream didn't come through. But he didn't let that crush him like it might have, considering how much of his heart and soul he'd put into the game since he was just a kid. He worked and worked and worked some more and made it to the majors as a teacher, and I believe he's the best in the business, a Hall of Famer at what he does. Beyond that, K-Long has a great, great family, and he loves, truly loves, what he does for a living.

If that's not living the American dream, I don't know what is.

CAGE RAT

1 | GREAT EXPECTATIONS

Football was my first love. That's right, football—eleven guys a side, not nine. I loved the camaraderie; I loved the hitting; I loved relying on my teammates and knowing they relied on me. But maybe the biggest reason I loved football so much was because of a coach.

Back in the mid-1980s, the football coach at my Phoenix high school—Thunderbird High—was a man named Owen Dejanovich. Coach D had played both ways at tackle for Northern Arizona University in Flagstaff in the early 1960s. The NFL Baltimore Colts and the AFL Houston Oilers drafted him in 1964, but he ended up playing for the Saskatchewan Rough Riders in the Canadian Football League. After his retirement as a player, he became an assistant coach at the University of Tulsa and then at Northern Arizona U before signing on as head coach at Thunderbird in 1985. I think you'll agree, that's a pretty strong résumé for a high school football coach.

Yet no way could I have guessed when I first met him that Coach D would have such an enormous impact on my life.

Even though I was a running back, and a good one, I don't remember any of the Xs and Os Coach D taught us. What I do remember, vividly, are the get-togethers he threw for the whole team at his house every

Thursday night during the season. I'm still amazed that week in and week out, Coach D's wife, Lesley, cooked for forty always-hungry high school football players. See, Coach D wanted us to be better football players, but he also wanted us to be better people who would work together, give strength to one another, help one another grow up, and—most important to Coach D—become like family to one another. He cared about us as people more than as athletes.

For a bunch of teenagers with a ton of energy, some talent, and no idea how to focus either, you couldn't ask for a better coach than Owen Dejanovich.

My father, though, was my first and strongest coaching influence.

Dad—Gary Richard Long—grew up in Van Nuys, California, which is where I was born on December 30, 1966. (Ever get a single present from some relative with "Merry Christmas and Happy Birthday" on the card? Then you know what it's like to be born during the holiday season.) My little brother, Timmy—excuse me, make that Tim; he's on the other side of forty now—came along two years later. My mother, still Donna Jane Carr when she and Dad met at the University of Arizona, was a housewife and boy wrangler; Timmy and I were quite a handful.

Dad started college at the U of A but finished up at Cal State Northridge. In 1972, the family moved back to Arizona where Mom and Dad, who is a CPA, built a solid middle-class household. In the summer of 1985, just as I was getting ready to go off to college, Timmy and I got a bit of a jolt when Mom and Dad decided to separate. A few years later they divorced. Mom got remarried to John Van de Water. She's still one of my biggest supporters. Dad remarried a great woman, Betsy Martens, in 1989. Currently, he's the CFO of a private company involved in automotive and real estate ventures in Phoenix.

Dad played baseball and football in high school, but he says that he was "only average" in both sports and never had to shuck any illusions about making his living from either. His one claim to sports fame, he says, is that Tom Selleck was a teammate of his on the Grant High baseball team.

For four decades and counting, Dad's been my best friend, my best coach, and my biggest booster, so naturally enough I consulted him frequently while pulling together this book. Good thing, too, because Dad remembers more about my life in sports than I do. And anything he was fuzzy about, he just looked up in his "Kevin Archives," the boxes of newspaper clippings, awards, and oddball memorabilia he accumulated while I was busy learning to go with the pitch from some nasty left-hander.

Here's one of Dad's favorite stories, one he's told, oh, maybe a hundred times:

When Kevin was nine or ten years old, we went with a family friend to an indoor batting cage so that Kevin could hit some balls. As we were finishing up, the owner of the cage came up to me and asked me how old Kevin was. I told him, and he said, "Whatever you do, don't let anybody mess with him. He has one of the best swings I've seen in a long, long time."

Later, when we were walking out to the car to go home, our friend turned to me and asked, "Do you know who that guy talking about Kevin's swing is?" "No," I said. "Am I supposed to?" "That guy," our friend said, "is Babe Dahlgren, the man who replaced Lou Gehrig at the end of his streak."

Dad spent a lot of time with me from the time I could hold a bat in my hands. He'd take me to the park and pitch to me, and pretty soon we'd draw a small crowd of people watching this little kid hit line drive after line drive. I know now, as a dad myself, how proud he must have been. He encouraged me at every step, but never put a lot of pressure on me. I made it easy for him, I guess, because I was a good athlete. And he never let me get too down—or at least *stay* down—after my team lost or I had a bad game. "C'mon, Kev," he'd say. "Gotta shake it off. You did your best. You guys will get 'em next time. Hey, let's go grab a burger."

When I was growing up, my favorite team was the Dodgers. The Dodgers were the *only* team in baseball, as far as I was concerned. I dreamed in Dodger blue. Dusty Baker, Davey Lopes, Steve Garvey, Pedro Guerrero . . . I *loved* those guys. Then, in the middle of my freshman year of high school, my dad landed me a job as a Milwaukee Brewers batboy during spring training. Suddenly, there was a new heaven, and I was in it. These were Harvey's Wallbangers—Cecil Cooper, Gorman Thomas, Paul Molitor, Robin Yount, Ted Simmons, Jim Gantner, Ben Oglivie, all the rest. I especially loved the manager of the team, Harvey Kuenn, who took me under his wing. What a great team! That year we went to the World Series! The Cardinals beat us in seven games, and that was plenty tough to take for one fifteen-year-old fan watching on TV back in Phoenix. But they were my guys, no matter what. My favorite color is yellow, and my wife, Marcey, says that's because it's one of the Brewers' colors.

My guys pulled some crazy jokes on me that spring. Like once sending me up to the home plate umpire and asking him if he knew where the bag of curveballs was. Or another time somebody saying to me, "Hey, Kevin, can you go ask the ump for the keys to the left-handed batter's box?" Today, baseball is still full of pranks, and batboys still receive the brunt of them. But I knew that when Gorman Thomas gave me twenty bucks and asked me to buy him a couple of hot dogs from the concession stand, he'd tell me to keep the change when I got back.

Know what? Being a batboy for the Brewers that spring may have been the most fun job I ever had.

Dad's time spent coaching me and encouraging my enthusiasm for all sports paid off when I hit high school. My freshman year at Thunderbird I went out for football, basketball, and baseball. Unlike high school athletes today, back then we were encouraged to play more than one sport, and I honestly feel that each of the sports I played helped me in one way or another. *Team* sports, that is—I wasn't drawn to individual sports such as golf and tennis, and I wasn't fast enough to even think about running track.

My sophomore year, I minored in JV basketball and majored in baseball, in which I hit .494, third best in the state of Arizona. I was 39-for-78 going up for my last at bat, but I choked and grounded out to third base, finishing the year at .494. (Believe me, it was a while before I stopped reliving that last at bat.) My thirty-nine hits were a school record, as was my .494 batting average. (Not bad for a five-foot-nothing, 115-pound sophomore, right?) Hitting over .500 would've been amazing, but the way I looked at it was that my junior and senior years were still ahead of me.

I passed up football my sophomore year. Summer baseball lasted into the beginning of football tryouts, but an even bigger issue for me was that the coaches wanted me to play quarterback. I hated the thought of being the QB; I wanted to be a running back. But I soon found out that I really missed football, and I decided that no matter what happened I would be out there the following year.

Come junior year, my mind was made up: I was going to be the starting running back on our high school team. Problem was, my summer baseball team went to the 1984 Babe Ruth League World Series—by the way, we won it—and I didn't finish up until fall football practice was well under way. Decision time. My chances of making the team looked to be slim to none, especially since my coach was still ticked at me for blowing off the previous year. So the first week I got back, probably figuring to teach me to keep my priorities straight, he sent me out to run plays against the first team defense.

To just about everybody's surprise, including mine, I shredded it. I mean, I was unstoppable. I made the team—and at the end of the season, I was voted MVP.

Basketball was a different deal. I started at point guard, and I was fine at handling the ball and getting it to the open man. But I couldn't shoot a lick. That became so obvious so fast that my coach, Bob Noice, warned me, "If you so much as try to take any kind of shot but a wide-open layup, I'll yank you out of the game in a heartbeat." Mostly, I heeded his warning, but from time to time I couldn't resist throwing one up. I learned quickly that Coach Noice went through with his threats.

But by spring of my junior year it was obvious that baseball was becoming my number one sport. Everybody's expectations, mine included, were huge, and I vowed to myself that I would *not* disappoint them. I didn't. I ended up hitting .468 with 5 home runs. On top of that, I was growing some, and my weight was now all the way up to 140 pounds.

Now Coming to the Plate, Marcey Long

Kevin and I first met in the fall of 1978 when we were both starting seventh grade. I had just moved into the neighborhood and didn't know a soul at school, but it didn't take me long to learn that Kevin was one of the popular kids and very into sports. Who could have guessed that cute little blond boy sitting next to me in the back of homeroom would someday become my husband?

After weeks of smiling, giggling, and a little chatting in the back of homeroom, Kevin passed me a note to "ask me out." (That was the way we did it back in the pretexting Dark Ages.) Many afternoons, Kev would ride his bike—a yellow-and-blue PK Ripper, his pride and joy—over to my house. My two little brothers, Mike (four years younger than Kevin) and David (eight years younger), loved having the stud of the neighborhood around. Kev would let the boys take turns racing his bike so that we could get a little kissing in.

On our first real date in our freshman year in high school, Kevin's dad let Kev use the family car. Neither of us had a driver's license yet, just our learner's permits! We drove to downtown Phoenix (about twenty miles round-trip to the state fair) and afterward to the Hamburger Works for dinner. (Still in the same place. Still great burgers.) Wow, did we think we were cool. Gary definitely won our votes that night for Arizona Father of the Year!

We dated pretty steady until the middle of sophomore year when we decided—neither of us remembers (or admits remembering) whose idea it was—to start dating other people. We stayed friends even after we broke up. Kevin also stayed close with my parents; they loved him because he was so positive and upbeat. Sometimes I'd come home from a date and there would be Kevin, sitting on our sofa visiting with my parents.

During baseball season sophomore year, after we were no longer girlfriend-boyfriend, I was Kevin's Guardian Angel. That was a "girl thing" back then, something like a Secret Santa. You would leave gifts, food, and surprises for the guy you were "guarding" before every game. And then, at the end of the season, you'd present him with a scrapbook for the year. (Not so "secret," I guess, but we Angels did take ourselves and our guarding quite seriously.)

I decided to grow up quickly (in retrospect, a little too quickly) after my junior year in high school by . . . getting married. (Married?!) Kev called our house on my wedding day, spoke with my sister Lisa, and told her he was coming to the wedding to stop it. She pleaded and begged him not to. Kevin finally gave in and said he would stay away. And then, just before he slammed down the phone, he practically yelled, "Have your sister call me when she's single again!"

Well, five years later, in the middle of Kevin's senior season at the University of Arizona, I reappeared at Frank Sancet Stadium to watch Kev play—and to tell him I was single. After the game he sent his buddy Scott Erickson to find me and to deliver a message: "Kev has some business to take care of. He told me to take you for a drink, and he'll be along in a while to meet up with us."

Turns out the "business" Kev had to attend to was breaking up with his girlfriend! And boy, did we have a lot of catching up to do.

My senior year in football I was—there's no way to describe it without sounding like I'm bragging—simply awesome. Our record was 8–3, and I rushed for 1,000-plus yards and scored 15 TDs. In the final game of the season I carried the ball 15 times, gained 174 yards, and scored our only 2 touchdowns. Little could I have imagined at the time that this would be the last football game I would ever play.

To top off that great season, I was selected to play in the North-South All-Star Game. You have to understand, the annual North-South game between the best players in the state was a very, *very* big deal in Arizona high school football. Man, I would get chills just thinking about how exciting it was going to be hearing my name called out in the Skydome in Flagstaff.

But then, two weeks before the game, my dad sat me down. "Son," he said, looking me dead in the eye the way he always did when he had something really important to tell me, "you aren't going to play in that game."

Say *what*? For a couple of seconds, I thought he was putting me on. But then I saw that unmistakable look in his eye, and I knew he was dead serious. "Dad, please! Why? Why won't you let me play? It's the biggest game of the year! I earned it! Why can't I . . ."

"That's enough, son," he said. "It's not up for discussion. You're not going to play in the game, and that's final."

If I knew one thing about my father, I knew that when he declared something "final" in that tone of voice, then that was that: *finito*, end of story, let's move on. Even so, I just couldn't let this one go.

"But, Dad . . ."

"No 'buts,' Kevin." The man rarely raised his voice to me, but he was heading in that direction. "You're not playing. Period."

I didn't play.

And I never understood why Dad wouldn't let me. So when I started working on this book, I asked him again: Why? "Easy decision on my part, Kev," he said. "You were the only member on either team who had Division 1 scholarship offers in hand for another sport. And I knew that your future lay in baseball, not football. It just wasn't worth the risk to that future."

Postscript? The guy who took my place on the South team got his leg broken. Dad couldn't resist reminding me that it could have happened to me. I nodded and said, "Uh-huh, uh-huh," to Dad. But to myself I said, *No way. I'm too quick and evasive. I wouldn't have let myself get hit that way.* (Hey, what can I say? I was eighteen, and I knew everything, and then some.)

Well, that quickness and evasiveness didn't save my butt in basketball my senior year. Late in the season, I got free on a breakaway fast break. I was going up for an easy layup—not even Coach Noice could have possibly objected to this one—when *wham!*, a defender blindsided me with a flagrant foul *and* came down on my back. The impact was enough to get me carried off the court and whisked to the ER at Good Samaritan Hospital. I guessed the second it happened that this was a bad injury, and I was right: a compression fracture that cost me the rest of my basketball season and most of my baseball season.

Fortunately, I did manage to play in eight games at the end of baseball season, enough for college coaches to see that I was okay. And so, on the strength of the numbers I had put up in my sophomore and junior years, my scholarship offers and letters from schools around the country—including one from Princeton! Imagine, Bill Bradley and I might have lived in the A-dorm at the same time!—remained on the table.

But if you're Arizona-raised, then really the choice is easy: U of A or ASU. And if both your parents are hard-core Wildcats, the choices boil down to just one option, and I accepted it faster than a roadrunner can cross a highway.

That fall, I enrolled at the University of Arizona.

My major at U of A was baseball, with a minor in partying.

The baseball was great. We won the 1986 College World Series. I was the only freshman to earn a letter. And well, I was damn good at partying, too. But I didn't exactly earn a letter in going to class. In fact, at the end of that year, I had to go to summer school to earn enough credits to stay eligible to play baseball.

If there's one part of my life I could do over, if I could give myself just one retroactive mulligan, it would be for my first year and a half at U of A. Let me explain myself. The baseball, the girls, and the partying were all great. But my attitude and goals toward school . . . well, that's what I would do over if I could have that mulligan.

My son Jaron graduated from high school in May 2010, and he shows a lot of promise as a ballplayer. Better still, he shows a lot of promise as a student. He goes to Chandler-Gilbert Community College located in Chandler, a little shy of fifty miles from our home in Scottsdale. And I just hope and pray he looks at my example and follows these words of fatherly advice when it comes to mixing baseball, partying, and schoolwork: "Jaron, my man, do as I say, not as I did: play hard—but study harder."

Just before the 1987 season, we went to Taiwan for a tournament, and I killed the ball: five home runs in seven games, made the All-Tournament team. And when we got back home to Tucson, how did I celebrate? By blowing off my finals. All of them. Consequently, I flunked out.

Good-bye, University of Arizona.

Good-bye, Division 1 baseball.

Hello, Scottsdale Community College.

That summer, though, Coach Jerry Kindall called Dad to say that he was going to hold a scholarship open for me. Dad says, "I told him that you felt really bad about letting him and the team down, and that I was sure you would end up making us all proud." Dad was right on both counts.

In retrospect, having to leave U of A was the wake-up call I needed. I put up good numbers at SCC. More important, I put up *good enough* numbers in my classes for four-year schools to figure I was worth another shot. I got offers from all over, including big-time programs like USC, Texas, and Miami. Here's how Dad remembers it:

> The SCC coach, Jim Coveney, asked Kevin what he wanted to do with the stack of letters from various schools he had in his office. Kevin told him to toss them away unanswered. That stopped most of them, but several kept on writing and calling. The University of Miami was probably the most aggressive in recruiting Kevin. I spent nearly an hour talking to their assistant coach, and I ended up telling him that Kevin owed it to Coach Kindall to return to the U of A.
>
> Besides, I said, if he didn't go to class in the desert, what was he going to do with the beach twenty minutes away?

My junior and senior years at U of A, I bore down on the books (no Fs or incompletes) *and* the ball field: first team All-Pac-10 both seasons, second team All-America my senior year. We had a hell of a team in 1989; we ended the season ranked number one in the country. Sadly, we didn't make it back to the College World Series in Omaha; Long Beach State knocked us out in the regionals.

Near the end of the season, I tore up my ankle and couldn't play in the regionals. Years later, at a team reunion, Coach Kindall told a few of the guys, "We lost our heart and soul when Kevin went down. That's why we didn't get back to Omaha." That's still one of the finest compliments I've received in thirty years of baseball dating all the way back to Little League.

Thanks, Coach Kindall. I'm eternally grateful for the second chance you gave me.

How good was that 1989 University of Arizona Wildcat baseball team? A pretty good measure is the number of our guys taken in the 1989 Major League Draft:

1st Round: Alan Zinter, C (Mets). My roommate in college, Alan labored in the minors for *fourteen* years with seven organizations (some of them twice) before finally making it to the bigs with Houston in 2002, when he was thirty-four years old. He got into thirty-nine games with the Astros and another twenty-eight with the Diamondbacks in 2004, then it was back to the minors before he retired from baseball in 2006. Alan and his wife, Yvonne, were very special to Marcey and me. He now coaches in the Diamond-backs organization.

4th Round: Scott Erickson, P (Orioles). One of my best friends in the game, Scott pitched fifteen seasons in the majors (thirteen of them with the Twins and Orioles) for five different teams. He led the majors in wins (twenty) in 1991, his rookie season, when the Twins won the World Championship. He was selected for one All-Star team (1991), and he pitched a no-hitter (1994). Scott and his wife, Lisa, are still very close to our family. Scott was my road roomie, and someone I can never thank enough for all of his gen-erosity.

5th Round: J. T. Snow, 1B (Yankees). J.T. won six Gold Gloves in his sixteen-season career (ten of them with the Giants). J.T. and I have remained close throughout the years. His father, Jack, was someone I really respected. Jack always said that my wild side and J.T.'s reserved side would balance each other out. J.T. was my room-mate, along with Alan Zinter. And, yes, we ended up being great for each other.

11th Round: Trevor Hoffman, SS (Reds). That's right, *shortstop*. The guy who anchored our infield went on to become the all-time major-league leader in saves (601) and a seven-time All-Star while coming out of the bullpen 1,035 times with zero starts over eighteen seasons. Hoffy and I were co-captains at the U of A, and boy, were we good at finding trouble. Personally, I think his decision to retire after the 2010 season was a tad premature. I mean, Hoffy's only forty-there! Seriously, as recently as 2009, the man had 37 saves and a 1.83 ERA. I wonder if we'll see him in Senior League Baseball one of these years at his natural position—shortstop.

33rd Round: Todd Deveraux, OF (Yankees). Todd played two seasons in A ball in the Yankees system before leaving the game. Sorry to say that I've lost touch with Todd over the years. Sure hope he buys this book so we can have a shout.

Not too shabby for a single college team in one year, wouldn't you agree? Wait a minute. I almost forgot. We had one other guy go in the 1989 Major League Draft:

31st Round: Kevin Long, OF (Royals).

2 | NEXT STOP: THE BIG LEAGUES

The week of the 1989 Major League Baseball First-Year Player Draft—a mouthful, but it's the official name—I was just a little revved up. How high would I go? How low? What team? This was way before cell phones, so I'd given my dad's home number to the people running the show so that whoever took me could contact me. But no way was I going to sit around the house waiting; I'd go stark, raving mad. Dad and Betsy bought an answering machine just so I'd be sure not to miss "The Call." I mean, if a team called and nobody answered, would they take somebody else? Would I drop a notch on their list? Be passed over and forgotten altogether? Would the other teams blackball me for demonstrating my lack of commitment by not staying by the phone 24/7?

As you may have gathered by now, I was borderline crazy with the suspense. When the phone rang in our house around six in the evening that early June day in 1989, I set a new indoor land-speed record running across the den to answer it: "Hello, this is Chuck McMichael [the scout who drafted me] of the Kansas City Royals. May I speak with Kevin Long . . . ?"

Round number 31?

The 801st player taken overall?

Yes! Yes! Yes!

Where do I sign?

I was on my way.

The dream that had been growing in my heart since I had realized that baseball was *my* game, *my* sport, was finally coming true. All those hours of hard work were about to pay off. A major-league baseball team wanted *me*. The Kansas City Royals were going to *pay me money* to play for them. Hey, they'd even given me a bonus—$1,000—*just for signing with them*. How great was that?

Three days after hearing my great news, I began my journey to the major leagues. After kissing and hugging my family and Marcey good-bye—she was going to visit me later—I hopped into my jam-packed blue-and-white Chevy Blazer and headed west for California. In Los Angeles, I switched from I-10 to I-5 north, toward my destiny. A little over eighteen hours later, I arrived in Eugene, Oregon, at the team hotel of the Northwest League's Eugene Emeralds.

If you're scoring at home, that's 1,225 miles, and yes, I drove it in one eighteen-hour bite, powered by coffee and adrenaline, and interrupted only by a couple of rest stop naps. You might say I was fired up to enter my new life.

The first couple of workouts went by in a blur as I met my new manager, coaches, and teammates for the first time. From Day 1, the differences, big and little, between my old, familiar baseball life and my new one leaped out.

One tiny example still sticks in my mind. At Arizona, I never once heard Coach Kindall swear, not even so much as a "Damn!" But Paul Kirsch, the Emeralds' manager, threw in a four-letter beauty every other word. It didn't take me long to learn that cussing, chewing to-bacco, and ragging on each other in the clubhouse were practically mandatory for a professional baseball player.

Damned straight.

* * *

Opening Day!

On the way to the ballpark, I was filled with anxiety. Was I going to be in the starting lineup? Was I even going to play? My stomach churned as I entered the clubhouse, walked over to the bulletin board where the lineup card was posted, and, trying to look nonchalant, scanned for my name. And . . . *Wow!*

I couldn't believe my eyes! There my name was on the lineup card, hitting cleanup! I'd been playing baseball since I could walk, but I had never, ever before batted cleanup! And there I was, on my very first day in pro ball, listening to the PA announce to the whole world, "Now batting fourth for the Emeralds, the center fielder, number 3, *Kevin Long!*"

And then, on a 2–1 count, I smoked a liner off the right-center field wall for a triple. Next stop: the big leagues.

Sure, I knew I still had a lot to learn. I knew I'd have to pay my dues in the minors for a couple of seasons, just like all but a handful of the thousands of guys before me. But I also knew in my heart that it was only a matter of time before I'd hear the PA system in Royals Stadium boom out, "Now batting third for the Royals, number 3 . . . *Kevin Long!*"

(Three was my favorite uni number from the time I could swing a bat. I wore it from Little League right on through high school and college ball. I didn't learn until later that 3 was the number worn by a certain old New York Yankee, one George Herman "Babe" Ruth Jr.)

My roommates my first year in professional baseball were Chris Shaeffer, Buzz Ahern, and Jake Jacobs, all pitchers and all guys I really liked. We shared a two-bedroom apartment about five minutes from the park that cost us $450 a month. We listened to a lot of music, talked baseball, and drank tons of beer. We even saved our beer cans and filled a closet with the empties.

That first season with the Eugene Emeralds I was dynamite (despite the occasional beer). I know that sounds like bragging, and I guess it is, but it's true. Yes, it was only Short Season A ball, and I was playing with and against guys just like me, guys who'd been drafted that June. But I flat out tore the cover off the ball: .312 with a .427 slugging percentage.

Man, oh, man! Two years later, three years tops, I'd be putting on my Royals home whites in the clubhouse at Kauffman Stadium in Kansas City alongside George Brett, Willie Wilson, Bo Jackson, Danny Tartabull, and the rest of my new teammates.

What can I say? That's the way a twenty-two-year-old thinks after a great first season in professional baseball. Turns out, of course, it didn't quite work out like that, but I was so psyched back then about my bright future that I used my $1,000 signing bonus to buy an engagement ring, and I proposed to Marcey as soon as she met me in Eugene.

She accepted!

I was going to marry my high school sweetheart. Make that my *grade school* sweetheart.

Marcey's parents weren't too thrilled about it when we told them. They liked me and all, but Marcey had two small children from her first marriage—Britney and Tracy—and her mom and dad thought I wasn't quite ready to support a family. I knew better. Sure, I wasn't yet making the big bucks—only $800 a month before taxes, as a matter of fact—but it was only a matter of time, a short time, before we'd be in clover.

Major-league clover.

Oh, I should mention that Marcey accepted my marriage proposal with just one condition: "When you get done with your playing career, Kev, please tell me you'll never coach."

Sure, babe, whatever you say.

The best day of my baseball life (to that point) came toward the end of that rookie season when Royals farm director John Boles showed up at a home stand to look us over. He watched us at practices and for a couple of games, spent a lot of time huddling with the manager and coaching staff, and on his last day in Eugene, he called a team meeting.

He congratulated us for our hard work and our play so far. (We ended up finishing 43–33, second in our division.) He told us we had a lot more hard work ahead of us, but that was the only way to get where we all wanted to go. Then, as he was getting more specific about what it takes to become a major-league player, right out of the blue he told the whole team that "this young man, Kevin Long"—and he pointed right at me—reminded him of Lenny Dykstra, and that I had a good chance to make it someday.

I was floored.

I mean, I was really and truly, honest-to-God speechless.

At least until that night, when I called Dad and told him what Mr. Boles had said about me reminding him of Lenny Dykstra, about how I had a good chance to make it someday, and how I was the only guy on the team he mentioned by name, and . . .

Dad heard me out, told me he was proud, really proud of me, and really happy for me, but I had to keep things in perspective: "Kevin, remember, this is only rookie ball. You still have a long, hard climb ahead of you." In other words, keep working, and don't let your dreams distort reality.

That honesty was and is, I know now, the hallmark of a great father.

After my gangbuster season in Eugene, I was invited to play in the Florida Instructional League. Major League Baseball created the FIL to give an organization's most promising prospects a chance to play more games and to receive more hands-on instruction from the coaches, so this was definitely a good sign of where I was headed.

Unfortunately, I lasted only about two weeks before I had to go home because of bone chips in my right ankle. The team doctors told me that the injury wasn't serious, and that they expected a full recovery within a couple of months. Even so, rehabbing and sitting around not putting stress on my ankle made for a pretty long winter.

Fortunately, there was one super high point: on February 17, 1990, Marcey and I were married.

The best day of my life, baseball or otherwise, before or since.

Five days later, I said good-bye to my new bride, packed up the Blazer yet again, and shoved east from Phoenix toward Baseball City, Florida, for my first spring training. That was a great trip. My college buddies Scott Erickson and J. T. Snow were also heading to Florida, and we caravanned the whole way. We made a short educational stop in New Orleans to steep ourselves in the local culture—that is, we celebrated Mardi Gras. Next, we somehow ended up in Tallahassee, home of Florida State University, so we went out and enjoyed an evening Seminole style, and even worked out the next day at their baseball field. (Cut us some slack; we were pretty fresh out of college, remember.) Three days and almost three thousand miles later, we split up and headed to our respective camps.

Spring training went well, and I ended up making the Baseball City Royals, which was KC's team in the Florida State League. I was one of two players who skipped a league; the other was Brett Mayne, the Royals' number one pick in my draft year, 1989. Needless to say, I felt pretty good about how my new career was unfolding after that skip-a-league assignment. Married life was treating me well, too, and I was ready for the family to join me.

Marcey, the kids, and I found a tiny place in Lake Alfred, Florida— Dad described it as straight out of *Mayberry R.F.D.*—that we rented for $350 a month. I was now making $850 a month, so things were looking pretty rosy.

At least that's what I thought!

You might think that going as low down in the draft as I did would have tempered my enthusiasm for my future prospects just a little bit. Fact is, though, it didn't really bother me. Sure, I'd rather have gone up higher with my U of A teammates. But I knew enough about baseball history to know that a lot of guys who were drafted low went on to have really good major-league careers.

For instance, I learned many years later about a couple of shortstops who went in the *forty-third* round of that 1989 draft—twelve rounds below me!—and who went on to have pretty good major-league careers. Maybe you've heard of them: Jason Giambi and Jorge Posada.

Jason Giambi and *Jorge Posada* in the *forty-third round?*

Shortstops?

Okay, that's a bit of a trick. Teams do that a lot, use their late-round picks to take younger guys who they think show real promise. The bet is that if a team can persuade a player to leave school before graduation, and thus before he puts up really big numbers, they can sign him for much less money. In fact, Jorge didn't sign until the following year, when the Yankees took him in the twenty-fourth round of the 1990 draft with the idea of converting him into a catcher. And Jason didn't come out until 1992, when Oakland took him in the second round, by which time he was a third baseman.

What's probably boggling your mind right now is a mental image of Giambi, all six feet, three inches and 240 pounds of him, turning a double play at short. Me, too, until I started thinking about it. Couple of things here. First, Jason may have been a few pounds lighter back in his shortstop days. Second, you almost always find your best athletes on high school baseball teams at shortstop. The best example that comes to mind is Mickey Mantle, who was a shortstop in high school back in the late 1940s in Commerce, Oklahoma.

It took Jason three years to get to Oakland. It took Jorge a good bit longer to get to New York. He played in a combined total of nine games in 1995 and 1996, but didn't come up to stay until 1997, seven years after he was drafted, and he didn't become a full-time starter until 2000. The explanation there, of course, is that he had to spend extra years in the minors learning a new position, the hardest one to master in baseball: catcher.

Three years in the minors seems to be about the norm for players who go on to become big leaguers, even "can't miss" first-round picks. Makes good sense, if you think about it. First, there's the huge leap in talent from college (and much more so, of course, from high school) to pro; you go from being your team's MVP to playing with and against nothing but MVPs. Even the top talents have some work to do to acquire and polish all five basic tools—hitting for average, hitting for power, glove, arm strength, and speed—that every major-league team looks for in position players. There's also the hard work of just plain old growing up, dealing with a whole lot of temptations that look like a gang of fun at the time but that often seriously undermine a guy's pursuit of his goal. Plus you're getting acclimated to a totally different mind-set, one in which baseball is way more than a game. It's your livelihood.

But the biggest change, the hardest transition, the single most difficult adjustment facing young position players going into professional baseball these days is one that a lot of fans tend to forget. Can you guess? It's the switch from aluminum to wooden bats. Believe me, if you've spent your high school and college ball hitting with metal, those first few hundred cuts with ash are strange, very strange.

See, the sweet spot on a wooden bat is much smaller than on an aluminum stick. You can use the end of an aluminum bat, get jammed, and still manage to hit the ball a long way. With a wooden bat there's very little room for error: you hit it square on the barrel or you're lucky to get a weak dribbler back to the pitcher.

Player development in baseball is unique among the three biggest team sports. Think about it: football and basketball have colleges to do all the heavy lifting in terms of getting guys ready for the NFL and the NBA.

Organized baseball, on the other hand, has *seven* levels below the majors, seven rungs in the ladder to the big leagues:

Rookie

Rookie-Advanced

Short Season A

Low A

High A

AA

AAA

Some players, even some household names, take a surprisingly long time to work their way up that ladder to the top rung. A recent example? Phillies outfielder Raul Ibañez, a guy I coached some when we were both in the Royals organization. I knew him to be a crazy hard worker, someone who had the will to keep on grinding and keep on learning. Although Raul was an All-Star in 2009 who went on to thump us pretty good in the World Series, he didn't rack up a hundred-game season in the majors until 2001. That's *nine years* after he was drafted in the *thirty-sixth* round of the 1992 draft.

But I didn't think much about climbing ladders back then, because I figured I was going to skip a few rungs, and not spend too long on any single one on my way to the top.

That was my plan, anyway.

3 | THE GYPSY LIFE

Ever hear the term "minor-league gypsy"?

You know, a baseball player who spends years moving through the minor leagues, making stops here, there, and everywhere at each of organized baseball's classifications—except one?

Well, meet Kevin Richard Long, ex-minor-league gypsy.

Here's my basic travel itinerary for my eight-year minor-league career: Eugene, Baseball City, Memphis, Omaha, Memphis, Omaha, Memphis, Wichita, Omaha, and Wichita. Most off-seasons, Marcey and the kids and I went back from wherever we were living at the time to Phoenix every Thanksgiving, returned on Sunday so the kids could get to school on Monday, and then do it all over again for Christmas. Our parents stepped up big-time to help us with all that prime-time travel, because goodness knows we couldn't afford it on our own.

At least that was the cycle until 1997, when I retired three days before what would have been my ninth season in the minor leagues.

That last move in my career as a player really, truly hurt because I really, truly loved playing baseball. I loved putting on the uniform and running out on the field. I loved competing at the professional level against immensely talented players. I loved the camaraderie with my teammates. I loved the pure joy of hitting a line drive into the gap and sliding into second for a double. I loved hitting a 3–2 slider up the middle to bring in a guy from third for the winning run.

I loved . . . well, I think you get the picture.

One goal kept me grinding and pushing and working and fighting through injuries. That goal, of course, was to express my love of the game in a major-league uniform in a major-league ballpark. I was driven by the belief that I could reach that goal if I just kept driving, driving, driving. That I was getting closer, closer, closer.

So near, and yet so far. The longer you play in the minor leagues, the more you realize how close in talent to one another all the players truly are. Look, I played on the same teams with so many guys that went on to play in the majors. Were they that much better than me? Immodestly, perhaps, I must answer with an emphatic "No!" More consistent on a day-to-day basis? Okay, maybe, but if I just kept on driving, driving, *driving* . . .

My goal was one I shared, of course, with every single teammate in my eight years in the minors. And only a tiny number of us reached that goal. Most of us didn't. But although I fell into that last group, I have never once regretted a minute of the time I spent pursuing that goal.

Kevin Richard Long, ballplayer.

Has a nice ring to it, don't you agree?

The Kansas City Royals, who gave me the opportunity to chase my dream when they selected me in the 1989 draft, was (and is now) an absolutely first-class organization. The managers, the coaches, and the front office people whom I had the honor and pleasure of playing for were to a man outstanding professionals who gave every player a fair shot at making it to the top.

That's important, because it's not always the case. Many outfits throw low-round draftees like me onto the back of the bus and never give them a serious look, much less a serious chance. The reason's pretty simple, if you think about it. They spend big money on signing bonuses for their early-round picks, so those are the guys who're going to get the first shot at playing. Late picks spend most of the time filling out the lineup (you need nine to a side, remember?) or keeping the bench warm. Because I played hard and had just enough talent, I got a chance to start at each level in the minors. That might not have happened if I'd been in some other organization.

Thanks, KC. I wouldn't be where I am today without your support along the way.

The differences between the majors and the minors are, well, both major and minor.

Let's start with lighting. In most minor-league ballparks, at least back when I played, we outfielders should have drawn hazard pay for night games. (And almost all the games we played *were* night games.) Shadows and spots and just general dimness turned going after fly balls into an adventure. And it got worse over the course of the year: most ballparks took a "Wait 'til next year" attitude toward bulb replacement. Hey, you say, what's the worst that could happen, an E-8? No, the worst that could happen would be if a top center-field prospect were to be conked in the head trying to catch a "routine" fly ball.

But as lousy as the lighting was, the infield surfaces in minor-league parks made me happy that I was an outfielder. I'd rather be an outfielder trying to find a fly ball in the poorly lit night sky than a second baseman wondering which way a hard grounder was going to carom over the lumpy, uneven, patchy infields.

And then there were the clubhouses.

You see a lot of clubhouses when you play for five different teams over an eight-year span—your own, of course, plus a total of something like fifty more when you factor in the other teams in the league. Even fifteen years later, three words come instantly to mind when I think of them: *small, dirty, smelly.*

In the minors you're packed in like sardines. Some places threw up portable clubhouses for the visiting team, with all the amenities you might expect. That is, none. At other ballparks, visiting teams had to trek back and forth to a locker room that was half a mile from the field, not a ton of fun if you had to run that distance during a midwestern thunderstorm. Air-conditioning that actually worked during the height of summer? Always plenty of hot water in the showers? Water coolers certain to contain water that was actually cool? Enough towels? Soap dispensers always filled? Shaving stuff laid out? Yeah, sure. Certain towns we'd hate to go to on road trips because the stingy local management provided just one clubhouse guy, and half the time he worked the home *and* away side. No way the poor guy could keep up.

You have to have balls to play baseball. (Sorry, sometimes you get a medium fastball right down the middle and you gotta take a swing.) But not all balls are created equal. And now I'm not joking. "A baseball is a baseball is a baseball" sounds like a truism, but it doesn't happen to be true. Balls in the majors are wound tighter and are therefore much harder than balls used in the minors. At least they were back when I was playing. Honest, I'm not making this up. Ask any veteran ballplayer and he'll tell you the same thing: major-league balls jump off the bat better and go farther than minor-league balls. Plus minor-league balls stay in play longer than their major-league counterparts; umps aren't as quick to toss out a ball just because of a little scuff. Pitchers love a ball with a little nick here and a scuff there; it helps them get more movement on their pitches. As you can imagine, we hitters would prefer to see a brand-new ball put in play on every pitch.

And then there was the fine postgame spread waiting for us when we were so ravenous after a three-and-a-half-hour game that we could have eaten a horse. *Not!* Most of the time, when we were on the road, we got nothing to eat in the clubhouse. Zero. Zip. *Nada.* Or if we did, it was some greasy, nasty fast food that made Golden Arch grub look like four-star cuisine.

Summer 1990, Florida State League (High A), my first full season in the minors. Don't recall what town we were in, but I'll never forget the doubleheader we played one Florida-hot, Florida-humid Saturday in August. We were playing two because Friday's game had been rained out, but I swear there was just as much moisture in the air when we took the field as there had been the day before. And wouldn't you know it? The first game went eleven innings. When we got back to the club-house for a short break after the first game we found this delicious, nutritious spread laid out for us: saltine crackers and peanut butter, along with some stale popcorn. No fruit. No iced tea. Not even a single damned Coke.

You got to be shittin' me! Here it was, 90 degrees with suffocating humidity, and that's what we get to replenish our bodies between games? Oh, I almost forgot, they had milk for us to drink. *Uncle!* It's a wonder we didn't pass out during the second game, when the temperature notched up a few more degrees.

(Let me make one thing clear right here. The clubbies I got to know and respect in my eight seasons as a player in the Kansas City organization took good care of us and always did their best with what they had to work with.)

Flash forward to the majors, where steak, fresh fish, and sometimes even lobster—*lobster!*—are accompanied by fresh veggies, fresh fruits, and an array of desserts. The postgame spread alone in a major-league clubhouse is beyond any minor leaguer's imagination.

The winter of 1990–91 was a scary time for me. In November 1990, the Royals flew me from Phoenix to Kansas City to have surgery on my right shoulder. In early January, I had surgery on the left. Both had labrum and rotator tears. The injuries to my right shoulder came from swinging the bat, the left from throwing. My doctors said they were both probably triggered by too much weight lifting. Instead of getting strong and flexible, I'd gotten big and bulky. No ballplayer wants to undergo any kind of surgery on his shoulders, but I came out okay.

After I was released from the hospital, I stayed with Betsy's sister Tina in Liberty, Missouri. This was a great time for me to recover and get acquainted with a part of the family I didn't know well, and I was grateful for how comforting and easy Tina and her husband, Glen, made it for me those first few days after surgery. After a couple days I was back on a plane home to recover and get ready for the season.

The part of my stay with Tina and Glen that I remember best was when we went out to Royals Stadium (now Kauffman Stadium). It was the off-season, but we were able to talk a groundskeeper into letting us in. I'd been there several times before, but let me tell you, it was always something special to visit that place, still one of the finest ballparks in baseball, and see it all empty and quiet. To this day, Tina says, she gets tears in her eyes when she remembers the look on my face as I walked out onto the infield and looked around at the big, beautiful ballpark that I believed in my heart would soon be my home.

Spouses were allowed to accompany their husbands on two minor-league road trips per season. Not on the bus, of course—and good thing, too, or the divorce rate among players would have definitely spiked. Marcey would meet me on a leg of a road trip that wasn't too far from our home, leaving the kids with another player's or coach's wife. Next time, she'd be the kid-minder and some other wife would join her husband. Our spouses did this sort of co-op thing all the time. We were all one big family in a lot of ways. It was kinda cool.

By now, you won't be startled to learn that the places we bunked on road trips tended more toward Motel 6 than Waldorf-Astoria. Make that *Roach* Motel 6. After Marcey's first road trip, the shabbiness of our room almost made her turn around and drive home. From then on, she always brought a light blanket that she would lay over the motel's covers: "No way am I sleeping on those sheets."

Can't say I blamed her, but I pretty much accepted my fate and tried not to notice how squalid some of the places we stayed in those first two seasons actually were. I decided it was just part of minor-league life, and, in fact, it did get marginally better as I climbed slowly up the ladder to AA and AAA. And I told myself that everything would change when I got to the majors. Someday, I'd tell Marcey, we'll look back on all this and laugh. But we didn't do a lot of laughing then.

The bus rides on those road trips were definitely no laughing matter. Try *sixteen hours* from Memphis to Orlando. Rides of ten to twelve hours were commonplace. Try sitting jammed into a bus seat next to another player for a ten-hour overnighter and see how much sleep *you* get. (Do I snore? Don't know; you'll have to ask Marcey. But I can give you a Hall of Fame list of ballplayers you've heard of who *do*.) Keep in mind that we usually had to play a baseball game the very next day—or the same day, if we had a breakdown or some other mishap and didn't pull into our motel parking lot until 3:00 in the morning.

By the way, I'm not talking luxury touring buses like you see today with roomy, comfortable seats that recline, and outlets for laptops. I'm talking chartered crates decommissioned from Greyhound service because the AC system or shocks or both were shot. Not fun.

After a while, I got used to the occasional blown-out tire or engine failure that added three or four hours to an already long trip. Plenty of time to think about your K in the ninth inning with the tying run on second when you pile into the bus immediately after the loss and head out toward the next stop? Oh, yes. Getting pulled over for speeding? Not so often; our buses weren't up to it. Being belted by one of those hellacious summer storms the Midwest can throw at you, the ones that light up the night sky and scare the living daylights out of you? Ho-hum.

Once, during my first season, the driver nodded off and came close to turning us all into ex-ballplayers. But that happened only once: from then on, we'd always post somebody up front to talk to the driver and keep him awake. Sometimes, of course, the designated sentry would nod off, but in my eight years in the minors as a player and ten as a coach, not one of the hundreds (felt like thousands) of road trips I made was interrupted by a traffic accident.

Sure, there was that time one year in AAA when our engine caught fire somewhere between Columbus and Who-Remembers-Where. (The road trips blur together, and I was almost certainly trying to sleep.) No problem, we spent an hour on the side of the highway waiting for our replacement bus to arrive. When it did, we created a long line from one bus to the other and passed the luggage like "olde timey" firemen with buckets of water. No harm, no foul.

Occasionally, something out of the ordinary would make our day, like the time an owl smashed into the front windshield, shattered the glass, and sent the bus into a little hula at sixty-five miles per hour until the driver regained his composure. No problem. The driver duct-taped the remains of the window in place, and after fifteen minutes or so, we were off like Willie Nelson.

On the road again.

Most people look at professional baseball players and assume they're rolling in cash. If they're looking only at major leaguers, they're absolutely right to assume so. The *minimum* annual salary for a player on a twenty-five-man major-league roster in 2010 was $400,000. But hold on: the *average* annual salary in major-league baseball in 2010 was $3.4 million. More precisely (per the Major League Baseball Players Association): $3,340,133. Now that is *definitely* rolling-in-cash money.

But if you look at the *entire* population of men who are paid to play baseball, it's a whole different deal.

(Right here I'd like to tip my cap to Mike Ashmore, a *Hunterdon County Democrat* beat writer who covers the Trenton Thunder, the Yankees' AA affiliate, for a blog of his that contains a lot of the info on minor-league pay and expenses that appears in this section.)

Players in rookie ball make something in the neighborhood of $1,250 a month. For five months. That's right, the minor-league season runs only five months, and players draw salaries only when they're playing. As they move up the ladder—if they do—they get raises, of course. All the way to about $2,500 a month. A cool $15,000.

True, players picked high in the draft do get rolling-in-cash bonuses. Stephen Strasburg the number one pick overall in the 2009 draft, signed a $15 million contract with the Washington Nationals. Of that, $7.5 million was designated as bonus money. That's the biggest bonus of all time, by a lot, but all of the guys taken in the first few rounds get handed six-figure checks for signing their names. And Strasburg made all those zeroes look like a shrewd investment: in 2010, he put up a combined 7–3 record with a 1.30 ERA in AA and AAA ball before being promoted to the majors, where he went 5–3 with a 2.91 ERA. But then—and this is the kind of thing that makes you want to throw up—Strasburg hurt his elbow and had to undergo Tommy John surgery (a procedure to reconstruct the ulnar collateral ligament on the inside of the elbow joint). We won't see him pitch again until 2012, and that's if all goes well. The stats say that 85 percent of the pitchers who have Tommy John surgery come back just as strong as ever. But the fact is we may never know how good Stephen Strasburg might have been.

"I'm very blessed to play this game for a living," Strasburg said at a press conference the Nationals called in August 2010 to announce his surgery. "This is a minor setback, but in the grand scheme of things, it's just a blip on the radar screen."

And then came the clincher for me: "I want to be the best at everything. Right now, I'm going to be the best at rehabbing and getting back out here."

Man, you just have to *love* a guy with an attitude like that.

But players picked well down in the draft—say, thirty-first round, like a certain Yankees hitting coach we know—are going to get a token bonus, a few grand at most, if they get any bonus at all. About 90 percent of minor-league players never make it to the majors, not even for the proverbial cup of coffee. In the three, four, or five years they spend chasing their dream, they don't even make enough to pay the rent.

The size of a player's signing bonus depends not only on what round he's drafted in but what kind of leverage he has. A guy drafted with a year of college eligibility left does have some leverage. He can say, "No, thanks, I'll take my chances in the next draft," and maybe boost his bonus offer. Happens every year.

For instance, the Yankees have a relief pitcher in their system named Eric Wordekemper, whom they took in the forty-sixth round of the 2005 draft; he was the 1,391st player drafted that year. Going that low, you'd figure he'd get the token thousand bucks, tops. But Wordekemper had a year remaining at Creighton University, so he was able to work out a deal with the Yankees for about twentieth-round money. The Yankees reasoned that if he went back to school and had a great season his senior year, then he might cost them even more in 2006—if some other team didn't pick him first.

On the other hand, a player drafted as a college senior has no leverage at all. He either takes what he's offered, or he finds another line of work. A first baseman named Kevin Smith, taken by the Yankees in the thirty-ninth round of the 2006 season, had completed his college eligibility at Oklahoma, so he did get the token thousand-dollar bonus. That came to about $660 after taxes, enough to pay for his food and maybe a couple of movies during spring training. He struggled in AA with Trenton in the Eastern League in 2010. Stay tuned.

Things get a whole lot better for minor leaguers if they're named to their big-league team's forty-man roster: $30,000 in their first year on the forty-man, $60,000 their second year. Decent money, but not exactly rolling-in-cash money. And whatever the size of the minor-league paycheck, it has to stretch to cover some things that may surprise you.

Take bats. Yes, the organizations provide gear ranging from batting gloves to cleats to bats. But a lot of guys don't want to settle for just any old equipment when the stakes are so high—after all, killing it in the minors is the only way they're going to get to the majors. So they dig into their own pockets and buy whatever they think will give them their best shot—and a top-of-the-line ash or maple Louisville Slugger goes for $75–$80 a pop.

Clubhouse dues take another sizable chunk out of a minor leaguer's monthly paycheck: about $350 a month, plus tips in the low minors, more as they climb the ladder. They get good value. A table full of food—the "spread"—after batting practice and games (often the only decent, nutritionally sound meal they'll eat all day). Plus clubbies do laundry, run errands, and keep the clubhouse from turning into a pigsty. (No easy task: think college dorm room times twenty-five.) Speaking of dorm rooms, three, sometimes four guys typically share a cheap apartment to bunk in during the season. A good clubbie would be appalled by how the place looks two weeks into it, but the price is right—rent often ends up taking a relatively small bite out of a minor-league player's paycheck.

It's the sneaky things that add up, the things you don't think about when you start. An old high school teammate e-mails you and asks if you could get him and three buddies tickets for the game Saturday night. Great, it'll be terrific to hang out and catch up after the ball game. But guess who pays for those tickets? Not the ball club, that's for sure. People assume that one of the perks of being a professional baseball player is an allotment of free tickets to home games. Uh-uh. The player pays for those "house seats." The same is true in the majors, only the cost per ticket is a lot higher. There, at least, the player doesn't have to skip a meal to do a solid for an old friend.

You get my point: minor-league ballplayers pay a pretty stiff price bucking the 10-1 odds against their chances of ever fulfilling their life-long dream. And the monetary cost is nothing compared to the emotional toll the game can take. If you don't believe me, just ask Marcey.

Like most minor-league gypsies selected in the bottom half of the player draft, Marcey and I had *no* money.

My salary in 1989, my first partial season in the minors, was $800 a month. That came to $4,000 a year. No, I didn't flunk math in grade school. In the minors, remember, you only get paid in the months you play, and $800 × 5 = $4,000. My salary in 1996, my last season in the minors, was $20,000.

During that time, we had two, and then three, children to support—Marcey's kids from her previous marriage, Britney and Tracy, and our son, Jaron, who was born in 1991. So how did we do it? We scrimped and saved and struggled and scrimped some more. And we worked. Boy, did we work.

You have to understand that working on something besides your swing or your curveball during the off-season is the only way most minor leaguers can make ends meet. Especially guys (like me) who don't get a big signing bonus and who (like I did) have kids to support. True, Marcey did most of the supporting, in addition to way more than half of the raising. But I jotted down a partial list of the off-season jobs I had from the fall of 1989 through the winter of 1997, and I have to say they do make for quite a handsome (and extensive!) résumé.

KEVIN LONG
UTILITY PLAYER
REFERENCES ON REQUEST

CAR SALESMAN (PHOENIX): Remember the Yugo? God, I wish I didn't. My first job after Marcey and I got married was as a Yugo salesman. I made exactly one sale, at a *steep* discount. In 2008, the fiftieth anniversary of the introduction of the Edsel, *Time* magazine published a list of "The 50 Worst Cars of All Time," and the 1985 Yugo GV was "honored" as one of them. In its description of the Yugo, *Time* called it the "Mona Lisa of bad cars. Built in Soviet-bloc Yugoslavia, the Yugo had the distinct feeling of something assembled at gunpoint."

WAITER (WINTER HAVEN, FL): Marcey gave me an ultimatum in 1990 after my second season: find a job or else. She was working two jobs at the time, and I guess she got tired of finding me playing video games with the kids when she'd come home for a breather. I didn't want to test what "else" might mean, so I found a job pronto at the local Olive Garden. Left my spikes and cap at home, put on an apron, and started asking people if they wanted the spaghetti or the ravioli. I was a terrible waiter. I don't have the patience to wait on people, especially high-maintenance people. And the tips were lousy.

JOURNEYMAN CARPENTER (MEMPHIS): A disaster. Built wooden pallets all day. Monotonous? Look the word up in the dictionary and you'll see a picture of me building wooden pallets. Plus blisters. My first week's check was a little shy of $180 take home for fifty backbreaking hours of work.

TRANSPORTATION ENGINEER (MEMPHIS): Okay, what I really did was load and unload trucks for an outfit called Overnight Transportation. Got the job through a guy I met at church. A blessing! And three times the hourly wage that I got as a pallet builder. I liked the physical part of the job, I liked the gang of guys I worked with, and I could live with the paychecks.

GOFER AT HEAVY EQUIPMENT COMPANY (PHOENIX): Dennis Peed, Marcey's dad, was a great man. He died from a stroke in 2006, and Marcey and I miss him dearly. Dennis owned Peed Equipment, a Caterpillar machinery business, and there was always work of one kind or another to be done. I drove fifty-three miles each way to and from work. That made for mighty long days. Dennis always gave me a hard time about leaving him tickets to minor-league games but never to major-league games. I know he's got a big smile on his face looking down at me now. I really wish I could leave Dennis tickets today for a Yankees–Red Sox game at the Stadium. What an amazing man, who taught me so much.

SHIPPING ENGINEER (PHOENIX): Worked in the produce department of Fleming Foods loading pallets—thank God somebody else had to build them!—for shipment to grocery stores around the city. Another job I enjoyed and was good at. You had to work hard and efficiently, two of my strong suits. Decent pay.

HIT MAN FOR THE CIA (PHOENIX): Not the CIA you're thinking about. This was a dry wall company where I worked briefly doing demolition with a construction gang. This was the most painful off-season job I ever had. I say painful because this is when I broke three bones in my face trying to take down an old door frame with a sledgehammer. I took a mighty swing—putting everything I had into it—and was totally unprepared for what happened next. The head of the sledge hit the frame, knocking it loose, but then recoiled and slammed into my left eye.

I went down like someone who'd just caught a C. C. Sabathia fastball in the face. As I was struggling to get back on my feet and remember my name, the foreman barked out, "Take a five-minute break, Long, I don't see any blood." Thanks, boss, but can somebody get me outta here? *Right now!* I'd knocked myself silly, but I hadn't knocked myself stupid.

Next stop: the ER.

"We can't get you in right now," said a guy shielded behind a glass-partitioned admissions counter. "Sit down in that chair right over there in the waiting room, please, and a nurse will come by soon to check you out."

Soon?

"Look," I explained, in a tone of voice that made even me come to attention, "either I see somebody right now or I'm going to take that chair, and I'm going to throw it through that glass. Let me put it another way: if somebody doesn't get me back there *right now* and give me a shot or something, I'm going to tear this place up."

The admissions fellow got me right in. I guess you could say I got lucky: no life-threatening fractured skull. I did have a fractured eye socket and potentially career-threatening damage to my vision. But I ended up dodging that bullet, too.

Following surgery to put things back together, I was covered in bandages and sent home. Scared the daylights out of the kids. Scared me, too. And even when most of the bandages had been removed, it was pretty obvious when I showed up to spring training about three weeks later that *something* had happened, and it was a bit more than a shaving knick.

The farm director, Bob Hegman, took one look at me and without so much as a "Welcome back, Long. Did you have a good winter?" he practically screamed, *"What happened to you?"* I told him, and he said, "Fine. Okay. Now give me the real story. You got in a bar fight, didn't you?" No, man, I told him: "I swear to God it was just like I told you." And I showed him the workman's comp papers from the company.

As a result of the accident, I now wear mirrored sunglasses all the time. Sunny and bright, hazy and overcast, just about anyplace but inside. I'm not trying to look cool. It's that if I don't wear shades, my left eye waters and doesn't squint properly. But my vision still tests out 20/20. As the doctor who fixed me up told me, "You were just plain lucky you didn't lose that eye."

No kidding.

You don't see too many one-eyed hitting coaches at any level of baseball.

DELIVERYMAN (SCOTTSDALE): I drove around the swankier areas of Scottsdale and Phoenix delivering furniture for Morse Studio, a high-end antique furniture store. Back at the studio, I did everything from moving around floor displays to running errands. Funny, despite my experience as a Yugo salesman, they never called on me to sell a nineteenth-century British highboy.

BARTENDER AND OCCASIONAL DISHWASHER (CAVE CREEK, AZ):
Marcey was the general manager at an upscale Mexican restaurant in Cave Creek where she worked eighty hours a week. The only way I could see her was to go work for her. This job came in handy during the 2010 season. Rob Thomson (our third-base coach) and I did a guest bartending appearance at Sojourn's Restaurant in New York City at a party to help raise some money for a friend in need. Sorry, Joe, but Marcey was the best boss I ever had.

FOUNDER, DIRECTOR, AND SENIOR INSTRUCTOR AT A BASEBALL SCHOOL (PHOENIX): After I retired as a player and became a coach, Marcey pushed me and pushed me and pushed me some more to start a company utilizing the skills and experience I had learned playing baseball, so I did. I opened Longball Hitting Camp in 2000, and I ran camps every winter through 2009.

We targeted young ballplayers ranging in age from Little League through college. Longball was successful right out of the box: over those ten years, we averaged about two hundred campers a year.

We broke the kids into age groups. My coaching staff over the years included major and minor leaguers, high school coaches, and major- and minor-league players. The camper-to-coach ratio was always around four to one, outstanding for camps of this sort—and a whole lot better than what major-league ballplayers have. (Try fourteen to one for ML hitters.)

We always held Longball at one of three high schools in Arizona: Cactus Shadows, Pinnacle, or Kingman. Most years we had two sessions, one over the holiday break in December, and the other in January on the weekend leading into Martin Luther King Jr. Day. We never advertised except by word of mouth. Jaron was our de facto promotions director; he always got a lot of kids from his Little League, club teams, and high school teams to sign up for one (or both!) of the three-day camps.

The cost ranged from $125 to $225, depending on the length of the camp—exceptional value, considering the level of instruction we provided. Each camper got a T-shirt and daily lunch. The workday (and I use the word on purpose) ran from 9:00 A.M. to 3:00 P.M. I always held a raffle at the end and gave out great gifts to the kids, including signed balls, batting gloves, shoes, and so forth. At first, Royals gear; later on, Yankees gear.

The Longball camp kept me sharp and was a great way to give back something to the kids in the area. Plus it brought in a few bucks, which the family sorely needed, even though Marcey was making a good income by this time.

So why am I using the past tense in describing Longball?

Well, I didn't run a camp in 2010. The off-season after the 2009 World Championship had been especially draining; even I can run out of gas now and then. Frankly, as much as I've enjoyed Longball over the years, and even though I know I've helped a lot of amateurs who love the game and a lot of kids who went on to play in college, I don't know whether I will be continuing it in coming years.

After all, this gig I have with the New York Yankees is a full-time job—and then some.

The point I'm trying to make here is that Marcey and I kept on pushing and pushing and pushing some more because we were both dedicated to a single dream, my dream of being a major-league baseball player.

Unfortunately, that turned out to be an impossible dream.

4 | MY DREAM CHANGES SHAPE

I was done.

The end of spring training in 1997 marked the final out for Kevin Long, baseball player, and a whole new ball game for Kevin Long, hitting coach.

Three days before the 1997 season opener, I went to see Bob Hegman, our player development director and the man in charge of hiring coaches. I officially retired as a player from the Kansas City Royals organization, and I asked him about a coaching job.

Yes, I remembered my prenuptial promise to Marcey not to go into coaching once my playing career was over, and I was positive that she remembered it, too. Marcey had been with me every step of the way through the preceding eight years—in fact, Marcey had made those eight years possible with her sacrifices and hard work. No one knew better than she did just how much baseball meant to me, how much it was in my blood.

When I posed the idea of retiring as a player and maybe going into coaching after all, we both knew without having to say a word that this was a huge turning point in our lives. I could tell by the look on her face and the slight tremble in her voice that she was on the verge of tears. But Marcey pulled herself together almost immediately:

"Go for it, Kev. Go for it."

Could I have continued as a player at Omaha that season? Sure, I guess so, except that I was twenty-nine years old, beaten up, frustrated, and disappointed at where I was after eight years in the game. I had a family that needed and deserved more from me than the AAA-ball salary I was bringing home. But the toll on the family was more than just financial.

When I started thinking about writing this book, our daughter, Britney, told me that she had tallied it up and that she had changed schools *fifteen* times during the time I spent wandering the minors. Not fifteen different schools, thank goodness; we mostly spent the winters in Phoenix, so there was some continuity there. But fifteen times she left a school before the academic year was out and moved to another school in Memphis or Omaha or Wichita or wherever. Looking back, it feels like we moved so often that we shouldn't even have bothered to unpack our bags.

Finally, there was a series of injuries whose cumulative effect had me feeling like an old man at the age of twenty-nine. Injuries are part of the game; we all know that. But I have to say I might have had more than my fair share of major injuries during my eight years in the minors. I had rotator cuff surgery on both my right and left shoulders, two months apart. I had surgery on my right ankle. I had surgery on my right wrist (the only injury that cost me a year of playing time). I had a hernia surgery. Plus there was that time I was attacked by a sledgehammer.

But what really sealed the deal for me that winter of 1996–97 was a little scouting report I prepared on myself:

Speed: Average.

Arm: Average.

Power: Well below average. (Just 14 home runs in 671 games—in A, AA, and AAA ball.)

Hit for Average: My lifetime .273 sounded solid, but I knew the number was deceptive. I hit .295 in 154 games in A ball, .276 in 390 games in AA, but just .234 in 127 games in AAA.

Summary: Kevin Long has organizational value. All tools play out okay. Good guy to keep around and fill in where needed. Plays the game right and could be a coach someday.

My scouting report looked about like what you might have predicted eight years before for an overachieving thirty-first-round draft pick. I had topped out well short of my dream come true. Even so, if I'd been single with no family obligations, I might have gone on playing minor-league ball until I qualified for Social Security—that's how much I love the game.

But it was time to go, and I knew it.

"Those who can, do. Those who can't do, teach."

Ever hear that one? Sure you have. And don't think it wasn't on my mind when I decided to make my move into coaching. I hadn't made it to the majors. And now I was asking for a job teaching guys a couple of years younger than me what they needed to do to get to where I hadn't been able to go myself.

Fortunately, Bob Hegman believed in me enough to give me a shot. And fortunately, I was so excited about being given the chance to stay in the game I loved that I didn't give a second thought to how poorly prepared I was for what came next.

My very first taste of my new job put a sour taste in my mouth. The day I became a coach, spring training camp was about to break, and all the minor-league rosters would shortly be set. Those last few days of spring training are when front office people, managers, and coaches gather together to make difficult decisions about who stays and who goes. So there I was, the newest kid on the block, listening to these guys methodically dissect the career prospects of some of my best friends. It was a crash course in how tough some of these decisions are and how much it eats a coach's heart out to have to tell a kid that he's being let go and his dream will never come true.

The transition from playing to coaching was tricky. I was expected to separate myself from guys I had been hanging out with every day for eight years—my peers, my friends—and forge new bonds with the coaches, most of whom were in their forties and fifties. (As I mentioned, I was twenty-nine.) I didn't do so well with the first part of my transition: in fact, I would catch a lot of shit from coaches and front office people through the years for being "too close to the players."

Frankly, I didn't care. My whole reason for going into coaching in the first place was to help players, and in order to do that I needed to know them. Seemed reasonable to me back then; still does. I build trust with players through strong relationships and use that to my advantage—and theirs.

In the early days, it was actually a plus that I was closer in age to the players than to the coaching staff. I could relate to the players in a way that the older coaches didn't—I understood what they were going through, and that helped me communicate with them. That said, I had to be careful. I had to respect the line between player and coach. Going out with players for a few beers after a game wasn't in the cards. A coach is management, one of the primary decision makers in the process that determines whether a guy is moved up, moved down, or moved out. You can't party with a guy one night and the next day cast a vote on whether to send him down.

But to do my job the way I think it needs to be done, I believe I have to *know* the guys I'm working with. The only way to get there is by talking with each of them, staying in close touch, and finding out what, if anything, might be troubling them. You have to find out what's going on in a guy's life off the field in order to determine what could be affecting his performance on the field. I have to understand and know my guys as people, not just as hitters, if I'm going to be an effective bridge between them and the team manager.

Look, there's a fine line between getting to know a player well and trying to become his buddy. Fine. I know that line, and I respect it. But if I don't work hard to know a guy I'm trying to coach, then how am I going to help him do his best? Today, I'll sometimes say to Joe Girardi that so-and-so might benefit from a couple of days off. It'll have nothing to do with the guy's swing, nothing technical, but I'll know that something is nagging him personally or physically and that a little breather might ease the pressure, get him back in a good groove.

My first season coaching, the Royals started me out in extended spring training, a camp for young guys who have talent but aren't, in the organization's eyes, quite ready to make a minor-league team. I was hyper-anxious to make my mark in my new job, and I jumped feet first into the challenge of helping guys with their swings. Looking back, I know I was too aggressive, too eager to make changes right there, right then. I should have done a lot more watching before I started talking. But baseball isn't golf: no mulligans.

To this day, I can't believe how lucky I was to get to work with some of the talent the Royals had in extended in 1997: Dee Brown, Alexis Gomez, Norris Hopper, Juan Brito, Jeremy Hill, and Byron Gettis all ended up playing in the major leagues. My only claim to fame after that first venture into coaching is that I didn't get in their way.

My days in extended spring training didn't last long. In July, our Carolina League (High A) hitting coach in Wilmington, Delaware, took a scouting job, and I was moved up to take his place. Needless to say, I was really excited about the promotion. As with every other assignment I've had in baseball, I jumped all over this new job. To become a competent teacher of hitting, I knew I had to first become a dedicated student, which to me meant watching players hit—not only my guys, but guys on other teams as well—with all the intensity and focus I could muster. "Learn by looking." If I'd had a motto to guide me back then, it would have gone something like that.

Matter of fact, "learn by looking" still works for me. I've never stopped studying hitters, my guys as well as the other guys. The day I do, the day I think I can't learn anything more about hitting by watching players hit, that'll be the day I should be designated for assignment.

The first person I studied in depth was Barry Bonds. He played in that other league, of course, so I got to see him in the flesh only once, many years later, in a three-game interleague series with the Giants in June 2007. (I looked it up: Barry went 4-for-8 with 4 RBIs, 4 walks, and a homer against us. Not shabby for a guy a month shy of his forty-third birthday.) But I studied video of Barry's swing until I had a perfect mental image of that short, balanced, explosive cut of his that made him the best hitter in baseball. That image helped me form my own theories about hitting and the mechanics of the swing. (Thanks, Barry.)

But while I was rawer than a shucked oyster that first year, I had someone else to draw on besides Barry Bonds: a certain gentleman named Jerry Stitt, U of A's hitting instructor and outfield coach from 1978 all the way till 1996, when he became head coach. Coach Stitt was an incredible teacher who taught me invaluable lessons about the ins and outs of the swing. He put in ridiculously long hours, diligently working on my swing and those of my U of A teammates. I'll always be grateful to Coach Stitt for setting such a great example, not only in terms of his understanding of the swing but also in his work ethic.

Years later, after I was named the Yankees' hitting coach, Coach Stitt told a reporter that "the one thing that separates Kevin Long from everyone else is his competitiveness. He was always figuring out ways to win every at bat. I could always see in him—because of the way he paid attention and cataloged everything—that he had the makings of a good coach." I took that as high, high praise from a man I really and truly respect.

Thanks, Stitter!

By the end of 1998 I had just finished my second year as a hitting coach in Wilmington in the Carolina League (plus a short stint as interim manager after the manager there was fired). I really liked working one-on-one with hitters, but I had another thing in mind. Managing. That's right, managing. I felt like this might be my calling and wanted to give it a try. I spoke to Bob Hegman about it, and once again he and the Royals stepped up to the plate and gave me a shot. In 1999, I managed the Spokane Indians of the Northwest League in Short Season A ball, back where I started as a player ten years earlier.

What an experience! At one point in the season we won seventeen games in a row. That's a lot of winning, no matter what the level. It was a streak I'll never forget, and probably one I'll never experience again. I'm not being pessimistic; I'm being realistic. The two longest winning streaks in Yankees history are a nineteen-game streak in 1947 and an eighteen-game streak in 1953, both World Championship years. The longest winning streak the 2009 World Champion Yankees could muster was nine games. That's okay. Never mind about setting records for winning streaks; I'll take the World Championships.

We were Northwest League Champions that year and I was named Co-Manager of the Year. The standard manager's "aw, shucks" response after winning a title is "You can't win without the players." And the reason you hear it so often, even from guys who secretly think they *are* the number one reason for a team's success, is that it happens to be 100 percent true. Seven of my guys that year went on to wear a major-league uniform: Tony Cogan (P), Mark Ellis (2B), Jason Gilfillan (P), Ken Harvey (1B/DH), Mike MacDougal (P), Brian Sanches (P), and Kyle Snyder (P). We had a great team, with an especially great pitching staff for Short Season A ball. You don't normally see one team in the lowest rung on the baseball ladder launch five pitchers on to a career path that ends in the majors.

As an aside, I'd like you to take a quick look at the draft positions of these guys: two first rounders (MacDougal, Snyder), three from the first ten rounds (Ellis, Harvey, Sanches), and two twelfth rounders (Cogan, Gilfillan).

None, you may have noticed, from the thirty-first round.

Problem was, I wasn't cut out for managing at that moment in my career. Oh, I believed I could handle the job. But slogging up the long road from A ball to the big leagues as a manager was going to take forever, and I needed to move a little faster than that.

Good-bye, manager Kevin Long.

Hello, hitting coach Kevin Long.

In 2000, the Royals named me hitting coach of the Wichita Wranglers, their AA team in the Texas League. I'd played for Wichita in 1995, its first year in existence. I had the best season of my career there, hitting .292. Not as good as one of my teammates, Johnny Damon, who hit .343 and was named Texas League MVP before being called up by the Royals. But good enough to get me promoted toward the end of the season to Omaha, our AAA club. So I came to Wichita—came *back* to Wichita, that is—with a good vibe about the place.

I had an even better vibe about my new job as a teacher because I knew from the start that I was helping my players become better hitters.

How do you know something like that? The players let you know. They're standoffish at first. You have to have a sizable ego to think you can beat the incredible long odds and make it to the majors in baseball. Most players, even the twenty-one- and twenty-two-year-olds, think they pretty much know it all and that there isn't a lot left for them to learn. After all, they have a skill that has set them apart since they were Little Leaguers. That is, the ability to hit a baseball. But if you're careful not to rush them, not overwhelm them with tips, they start coming to you for advice—"Hey, Kev, am I getting my back side through all the way?"—and not waiting for you to go to them. Plus you know you're having a positive impact when you see guys start hitting better after they start putting into practice stuff you've drilled into them.

Take Brandon Berger. We had a good hitting team my two seasons in Wichita—a team BA of .280 both seasons, a pretty hefty team average in any classification. (Point of reference: the 2009 Yankees hit .283 as a team, second in the AL only to the Angels at .285.) Some guys definitely looked like they were on their way up, but Brandon looked like he had topped out. At least that's what most people thought when he hit just .163 in twenty-seven games after being promoted from Wilmington. The next year, though, Brandon exploded with a .308 BA and 40 homers.

This was a terrifically satisfying experience for me, and a perfect example of what I loved about my nine years as a hitting coach in the minors: taking a guy people had given up on and helping him get the most out of his natural abilities.

For the record, Brandon got called up to the Royals that September, and he played bits of three more seasons with KC before retiring as a player in 2005. I still keep in touch with Brandon, who currently lives in Fort Mitchell, Kentucky, and works at an indoor baseball facility teaching hitting.

I applaud his choice in second careers.

Things were going well.

The Royals had taken a big risk on an unknown quantity and given me a terrific opportunity to stay in baseball. I paid them back by working my tail off.

I knew they liked my work, because in September of 2002 and 2003, when KC and the major-league teams expanded their rosters to forty, I was one of the handful of Royals minor-league coaches to get a call-up to the big club.

All baseball fans know about September call-ups, when rosters expand from twenty-five to forty. Teams still in the hunt bring up fifteen additional players to give them more depth in the last month of the season. Teams playing for the next year use roster expansion to get a close look at their top prospects, guys who have a shot at cracking the top twenty-five when "next year" rolls around.

What a lot of serious baseball fans may not know is that coaches get called up in September as well, and that getting that opportunity to be with the big-league clubs matters a lot to us, too.

If you're a minor-league player, especially if you're early in your career, being a September call-up is a very big deal. It means that you've caught the organization's attention, that they think you have serious promise. At least that's the way players interpret it.

Well, the same is true for coaches. I was thrilled when I joined the big club in September of 2002 and 2003. To me, it meant that the Royals were looking me over, that I was on their radar.

So how come the cap I've been wearing since 2007 has NY on it instead of KC?

Pretty simple, really. Marcey and I were strapped financially, and the Royals couldn't come up with a big enough number at contract renewal time after the end of the 2003 season. I asked for permission to look elsewhere, and they graciously agreed to let me pursue other options. And so I immediately picked up the phone and called Bucky Dent.

In Boston, of course, he's still known as "Bucky F— Dent" because of the three-run homer he hit in the AL East Division playoff game against the Red Sox in 1978. In New York, he's remembered fondly for hitting .417 in the Yanks' triumph over the Dodgers in the World Series that same year, for which he was named MVP. But to me, he is simply Bucky Dent, friend.

Bucky and I had worked together in AAA Omaha in 2002 when he was manager and I was hitting coach. We became very close friends that season and formed a bond for life. I respect Bucky a great deal, and I've always regarded him highly as a savvy baseball man. The reason I mention Bucky here is because when the Royals and I parted ways, Bucky spoke to people he knew in the Yankees' front office about me and told them what an asset he thought I would be to the organization.

A few days later I got a call to come in for an interview with Gordon

Blakely, who ten months earlier had been named senior VP for baseball operations with the Yankees. We met, talked for a good long while, and I thought it went pretty well.

And then, on November 10, 2003, I got a follow-up call.

"Kevin, this is Mark Newman. I'm the vice president in charge of player development of the New York Yankees . . ."

Oh, my God! Could it be? Could it really be . . . ?

" . . . and I'd like to talk to you about coming to work for us."

5 | NOW COMING TO THE PLATE, MARCEY LONG

On Saturday, August 19, 1989, I flew from Phoenix up to Eugene, Oregon, to visit Kevin, who was playing his first season of professional baseball with the Eugene Emeralds, a Kansas City Royals farm club. He met me at baggage claim, and we exchanged a big kiss, the kind that two young people in love who haven't seen each for a while specialize in. I was expecting to go straight from the airport to his apartment to change out of my trendy Hammer pants and matching jacket (hey, it was still the '80s), but Kevin said he wanted to stop somewhere else first. Sure, I said, okay, and he drove us to a park on the Willamette River, where he had rented a canoe.

A canoe? I looked down at my four-inch spike heels and thought, *Damn, how's this going to work?* But I stepped as gracefully as I could into the bobbing canoe, while refraining from asking any questions or saying what was really on my mind. (I had different ideas of how and where we were going to rock the boat that afternoon.)

Kevin rowed us downriver to a shaded grove along its eastern bank. Once he found his perfect spot under a giant willow tree, he got down on one knee as best as he could in the boat, and he took my right hand in his and asked me a question:

"Will you marry me?"

"Yes! Yes!" My answer tumbled out while the words were still coming out of his mouth. Romantic? Oh, my, yes. We were married six months later on February 17, 1990—*before* spring training camp opened, of course—in Phoenix.

I had found our hero, one for my two kids, Britney and Tracy, and one for myself.

Our first home together as a baseball family was a tiny duplex in Lake Alfred, Florida, near the Royals' farm club in Baseball City. We were two thousand miles east of our nice, three-bedroom house in Phoenix, two thousand miles east of our family, two thousand miles east of everything comfortable and familiar in our lives. Kevin was on the road half the time, and I worked my tail off turning our little house into a home. The only possessions we brought with us were whatever we'd been able squeeze into the U-Haul trailer hitched to our car. Unfortunately, the kids' bikes didn't make the trip; there just wasn't enough room. The kids were so, so sad at first and having such a hard time adjusting to their new lives with no bikes and no grandparents next door. We couldn't do anything about the grandparents, but the kids and I searched garage sales until we found some good, affordable used bikes. That pattern of leaving bikes behind us in Phoenix and finding new ones in each new city continued throughout our years in the minor leagues.

Thinking back, I can laugh at how shabby and poorly furnished our first place was. All I can say is that it's a good thing we were young and in love, so that sort of thing didn't matter much. The mattress on our double bed in the "master" bedroom was so sunken in that my mom told me, "If you don't get pregnant here, you never will."

Good call, Mom.

Nine months later, Jaron Richard Long joined our little family.

* * *

Beginning with that first minor-league season with the Baseball City Royals in Florida, I always made it a top family priority to find us a church right away, wherever we went, because I felt that it gave us stability and a sense of community. Some of our best friends in baseball have come our way through the churches we've attended while stationed away from Phoenix. Those friends in our minor-league stops became our "other" family. For instance, a kind man we met in church that first year worked for Disney World, and he gave us his family passes to the park. We pretty much lived there and at the beach.

I had three jobs that first year. During the day I worked at Tracy's private Christian preschool; the job paid just enough to cover his tuition and not much more. During the evening, I worked at a local steakhouse, one of those places where the principal draw was its all-you-can-eat buffet. My polyester uniform—my least favorite among several uniforms I would don over the next few years—was an unpleasant shade of "forest green." The pay and tips were even lousier than the uniform, so I soon moved on to a job as a cocktail waitress. At the cocktail lounge I wore stilettos, a black leather vest, and black fishnets.

From forest green polyester to black leather and fishnets? Dynamite! Especially since I was making a ton more money serving martinis and mai tais than I'd brought in stacking buffet dishes. But just as we were getting used to the extra cash, I found out that I was pregnant. I was worried that they wouldn't let me keep working there when I started to show, but luckily I didn't have to worry long: Kevin got called up to Memphis, and we hit the road.

Once, when I was still working at the steakhouse, Kevin brought a camera along on a night he and the kids came in to eat. Tracy had seen me in uniform there before and wanted a picture of me wearing it. He thought it was as cool to see me in *my* uniform as it was to see Kev in *his*. The only place that was going to happen was at the steakhouse itself, because I always changed into and out of the ugly thing there. Bad enough that I had to wear it. Even worse if I'd had to wear it out on the streets.

Kevin and I both thought it wouldn't be such a hot idea for the kids to see my cocktail waitress getup, so there's no photographic record of the stilettos, the little leather thing, and the fishnets. Too bad.

The kids and I went to a ball game just about every night that first summer in Baseball City. We didn't have the money to do much of anything else, and it was very social for us. The other wives and kids formed one big extended family. There were never many fans at these games partly because it was Class A ball, but mostly, I think, because of the gigantic mosquitoes that thrived in that stretch of sweltering southern Florida. The ushers and the concession workers knew all the kids, so the popcorn was free. One of the ushers would give the older kids a walkie-talkie, so that the whole pack of kids could pretty much have free run of the complex.

At our next stop, Memphis, the kids had to sit in the seats. After all, we were in AA ball now. But the moms always brought along plenty of toys, so the kids didn't have to follow the action on the field—except, of course, when their daddies came up to the plate.

The summer of 1991, Kevin left for Memphis after being held back in extended spring training while he continued to recuperate from two shoulder surgeries over the preceding winter. Four months' pregnant and with two young kids in tow, I packed our stuff into a U-Haul, and away we went, leaving Florida to meet Kevin in Memphis. Kevin's stepmother, Betsy, is from Memphis, and most of her family still resides there, so we stayed with them until we found a nice little two-bedroom apartment.

Memphis was my favorite of the many stops in Kevin's minor-league career. That cliché you always hear about "southern hospitality"? Well, it's no empty cliché. It's true. We experienced it firsthand. We met some great people and made some great friends *outside* the baseball community. Betsy's family treated us as their own, and the folks we met in our neighborhood and at church were just so genuinely nice. And let me tell you, you haven't eaten Easter dinner until you've eaten it in the South!

One thing that I discovered during our travels through the world of minor-league baseball is how cultural food can be. The kids associated each state with the popular cuisine du jour. At a young age they were downing—and loving—raw oysters in Florida, eating black-eyed peas and grits in Memphis while answering "Yes, ma'am" and "No, sir," and devouring rhubarb and sweet corn in Nebraska. I always aimed to be consistent with mealtime. To me, that's family time, not eating-while-sitting-in-front-of-the-TV time. Whenever we ate, we would sit together at the table and enjoy conversations about our days.

Even though Jaron was only six weeks old, I went out and got a job shortly after the season ended. I had no choice; we needed the money. So I became the most reluctant waitress in the entire history of the Perkins Restaurant and Bakery chain. That Perkins job was my least favorite in all the years we spent scuffling around trying to make ends meet: nonstop work, crazy long hours, lousy pay, and back in polyester—but the tips kept us afloat through the off-season.

Kev had had a solid season in Memphis. We figured he might get moved up a notch, so we stayed put through the winter rather than return to Phoenix. After all, there are only so many times you can pull up stakes and move in a single year, right? Sure enough, Kevin got the news midway through the following spring training that he was being promoted to AAA ball in Omaha.

Great news! I packed up yet again, and off we went. I was excited to be making a move to the Midwest. This is where I was born and spent a small chunk of my childhood, and I still had family in the area that we could count on and visit. I can never thank my uncle Tom and aunt Rhonda enough for supplying us with a car every season in Omaha, for always being ready to take us out for a great meal, and for still making it possible for our family to make Thanksgiving visits every year to a place we called home once upon a time.

Three moves in three years, the last one with two school-age kids and an infant. Makes me tired just remembering, and it was only the beginning.

That year in Omaha we rented a really nice house from Brian Poldberg, a Kansas City coach, and his wife, Lori. It was like a palace compared to our first two places. Jaron had a beautiful nursery! Brit and Tracy had their own rooms! Plus there was one other huge bonus that summer: Kevin's grandmother ("Grandma Jane") came out from Phoenix and stayed with us. Boy, was I glad to have another adult in the house, and some help with the kids, especially when Kevin was on the road.

After the 1992 season, a really discouraging one for Kevin, we moved back to Phoenix. Kevin helped pack up for the first time; I think it made him appreciate me more. My parents rented us the house I grew up in, and I got another job waiting tables, with Grandma Jane making everything possible as my right-hand lady. Her invaluable presence helping with the kids also freed up Kevin to get one of his crazy off-season jobs.

Kevin learned after only a couple months into the 1993 season in Omaha that he was being sent back down to AA in Memphis. That hurt, but Kevin was—still is, always will be—a fighter. He reacted to the news, at least outwardly, as if it were just a bump in the road. I don't remember him ever complaining, whining, or getting down on himself. Originally, I had been set to meet Kev, kids in tow, in Omaha at the end of the kids' school year. That way, we'd have plenty of time to find a place in Kansas City. (Dare to dream!) But when it turned out that Kev would be going back to Memphis, I decided to stay in Phoenix with the kids and keep working and then come out for the summer.

So that's what I did. But, midway through the season, Kevin was promoted back up to Omaha. We all missed each other so terribly that I packed up only enough clothes and toys to survive, and off we went to meet him. We lived in another tiny two-bedroom apartment and quickly got back into our baseball routine. At the end of the season, we headed back to Phoenix where our old, familiar house was waiting, along with an old, familiar school for the kids.

And my off-season job? A new one for me: bartender.

Let me tell you, bartenders make a lot more in tips than waitresses. What'll it be? The usual?

After missing most of the 1994 season with a wrist injury, Kevin was assigned to the Royals' farm team in Wichita, Kansas, for the 1995 season. He'd hoped to stay in Triple A; the Wichita Wranglers were a step back down the ladder. Kev didn't blame anyone else or outside circumstances; he took it on his shoulders like the stand-up guy I've always known him to be. I admired him, but I also had to wonder, where were we going? I had told him a long time before, and I remember my exact words, "You can play as long as you can, and I'll do my best to support us. But we both have to be realistic, and when it's over, even if you've never made it all the way to the majors, you have to see that, accept it, and move on."

I did *not* want to have a couple of teenagers changing schools every six months or so the way we had when they were little. And I was explicit about one thing: no coaching. What it came down to is that I did *not* want to be a minor-league coach's wife, working full-time at one if not two jobs to make ends meet, while raising two teenagers and a little one. I got Kevin to confirm his promise to me that summer of 1995 that that would never happen.

No coaching.

* * *

The 1995 season was a very difficult one for the family. In June, only days before I was going to pack up the kids and head to Wichita, Kevin called: "Good news, babe! They're sending me up to Omaha. I'm leaving in an hour. Meet me there."

Frankly, I hadn't relished the idea of going to Wichita. I knew I wouldn't find a very happy man there. But Omaha was a different thing. He'd been promoted, and he was excited. Me, too. I found a nice place there pretty fast. (I was a pro at this by now.) Once we were settled in, I called my parents and gave them the green light to come on out. They came to visit us every summer no matter where we were living.

But, a couple of days later, with my parents in the plane on their way from Phoenix and no way to reach them, Kevin called me from the Omaha clubhouse and dropped a little bomb on our plans: "Babe, change of plans. I hate to tell you this, but they're sending me back to Wichita."

Oh, no!

Here we go again. But this time I sure wasn't going to pack up, drive back to Wichita, and go through the whole routine of renting yet another place again. So I called the apartment rental agency and told them we were leaving; next I called to have the utilities shut off; and I started packing up again.

Fortunately for me, my parents would be around to help me load the U-Haul.

Destination: Phoenix.

Wichita was not in the cards for the kids and me.

But then, the very next day, after I had notified the rental agency, canceled all our utilities, and packed up the U-Haul with my parents' help, I got another call from Kevin: "Babe, don't move after all. A guy got hurt and they're keeping me in Omaha."

Okay, good. I'll just tell the apartment rental agency and we'll move back in. But this time the agency insisted that I sign a six-month rental agreement. I had no intention of spending Thanksgiving in Omaha, thank you very much. So I found another place the same day—smaller, not as nice, but a month-to-month deal.

Somehow, everything worked out. I got the utilities and phone up and running, and I had my game face on when Kevin got back from his short sojourn in Kansas. We were a nuclear family once more. But not for long: ten days later, Kevin got the word that the Royals were sending him back to—yes—Wichita.

That was it for me.

Three days later, the kids and I pulled into the driveway of our home. In Phoenix.

Kevin started the next season—that would be 1996, if you've been following our long and winding trail—in Wichita. This time the kids and I stayed back in Phoenix, end of discussion. We certainly didn't want to yank the kids out of school in the middle of the second term, and we wanted to see how things would go for him in Wichita.

The upside: Kevin got off to a solid start with the Wranglers. I was managing a restaurant and making pretty decent money. We bought our first home. Grandma Jane took care of the kids while I worked. Britney was now in sixth grade; this would be the first time she'd ever completed a year at one school!

The downside: Kevin and I really missed each other, and the once-a-month visits we had planned were expensive, disruptive, and not enough time together. Kevin spent the whole season in Wichita. Good numbers, but no promotion, not even back to Omaha, much less to Kansas City.

That off-season, we were both crazy busy with jobs and raising three kids, and we didn't talk about Kevin's baseball future. What was there to say, anyway? Kevin turned twenty-nine on December 30; he'd been in the minors eight years. So I can't say I was all that surprised when, near the end of spring training the following March, I got a call from the Royals camp:

"Babe, we need to talk . . ."

*   *   *

I was emotionally prepared for what I felt sure was coming next: Kevin had decided to give up a dream he'd had since even before I first met him back in junior high.

He was going to retire from baseball.

Since that beautiful summer day on the banks of the Willamette River nearly eight years before, our deal was that Kevin could keep on playing baseball as long as he wanted, keep on trying to get to the majors. But the majors were getting farther away, not closer. The kids would soon be teenagers. They needed stability. It would be tough enough for them without us moving every year or so.

But I wasn't prepared for his actual words: "Babe, we need to talk about me taking a coaching job."

Coaching wasn't part of our deal. The money for minor-league coaching was just plain lousy. How could we possibly put enough away to send three kids to college? We'd still be moving from one minor-league town to another every year or so . . . Kevin would still have to be on the road half of every summer, leaving me to raise the kids alone . . . and I'd still be saddled with being the family's principal breadwinner.

Coaching? I thought we'd agreed that was never going to be part of our future together.

And so we had. But my hero had just had his lifelong dream shattered. He had lived and breathed baseball since he could hold a bat in his hands. He didn't know how to do anything else. His *life* was baseball. And the only way he could continue that life was to become a coach. He was still our hero, but his dream of playing in the majors was never going to come true. Now he wanted a chance to prove that he had what it took to help other young ballplayers fulfill *their* dreams.

This was a turning point in all our lives. At this time, I was running a restaurant and supporting the family financially. Sure, I had to put in fourteen-hour days—thanks again, Grandma Jane, for making that possible—but we were doing okay. If he would just come back to Phoenix, I knew he could find something that would engage him. Maybe coaching in high school? Maybe something outside of sports altogether?

That's what my head said. But my heart said that I needed to support my hero in his *new* dream.

My head said, *No way.*

My heart said, *Yes, Kev. Go for it. Give it your best shot.*

Today, I am so very, very happy that I listened to my heart.

6 | "HITTING COACH, NUMBER 54, KEVIN LONG . . ."

The Voice of God."

That's how Reggie Jackson once described the sound that rolled out over Yankee Stadium when the legendary Bob Sheppard, the Yankees' announcer for fifty-six years, introduced the complete rosters of both teams, including managers and coaches, at the home opener every year. Even if the Yankees opened on the road, everyone said, the season wasn't officially under way until Mr. Sheppard had completed his work and Robert Merrill had sung the national anthem.

Mr. Sheppard's tour of active duty ran from 1951, Mickey Mantle's rookie year, through 2007, my rookie year as the Yankees' hitting coach. He was ninety-seven that spring, and he spent the next two seasons (2008–09) on the DL before he officially retired in October 2009. I felt deeply honored and in absolute awe when I met him that first summer. There he was, in person: the Voice of God.

On Monday, April 2, 2007, at 12:59 P.M., when the words "Hitting Coach, Number 54, Kevin Long" swept over Yankee Stadium from the Voice of God—excuse me, Mr. Sheppard—I practically sprinted out of the dugout to join my new team along the first-base line. The only reason I didn't somersault all the way is that I would have busted my butt.

Mr. Sheppard's death on July 11, 2010, was a blow to all Yankees and Yankees fans. And the fact that Mr. George Steinbrenner died two days later—the day of the 2010 All-Star Game—meant that within forty-eight hours we lost two great Yankees All-Stars.

How does a team honor a legend like Mr. Sheppard?

It started back on May 7, 2000. In celebration of Mr. Sheppard's fiftieth season as the Yankees' PA announcer, a plaque identifying him as "The Voice of Yankee Stadium" was installed in Monument Park at the Stadium. (Walter Cronkite, who had a pretty recognizable voice himself, served as the public address announcer during the ceremony.)

On July 14, 2010, the Yankees announced that players and coaches would wear a Bob Sheppard commemorative patch on the left sleeve of their home and road jerseys for the remainder of the 2010 season. And on July 16, 2010, at our first home game after Mr. Sheppard's death, there were no public address announcements at all and the PA booth was left empty.

But to me the greatest honor to Mr. Sheppard came back in 2008 when Derek Jeter asked him to record his at-bat announcement so that it could be used to introduce each of Jeet's home at bats for the rest of his Yankees career. (At the 2010 All-Star Game, Mr. Sheppard's recording was also used to introduce Derek when he came to bat for the American League in the bottom of the first.)

Derek's request rendered Mr. Sheppard speechless. Well, almost speechless: "It has been one of the greatest compliments I have received in my career of announcing. The fact that he wanted my voice every time he came to bat is a credit to his good judgment and my humility."

When I think of the marvelous sound of that great gentleman's voice and the *feeling* I got hearing it—well, my goose bumps had goose bumps. This was the moment I'd waited for my whole life, to hear my name announced in a major-league baseball park. My emotions were so intense that the part of the day leading up to the game is a blur. That's okay. After I trotted out and took my place on the first-base line, Don Mattingly gave me a welcoming smile and patted me on the back.

I belonged.

I was home.

Really, no words can adequately describe my feelings on Opening Day 2007 in Yankee Stadium.

Those eighteen years in the minor leagues had finally paid off. I couldn't believe that my first job in the majors was with, of all teams, the New York Yankees. What an honor! An honor I'm so, so grateful for. Nervous? Not really. More like busting with pride and excitement. All I could think about were the many places Marcey and I and the kids had lived over the years, as I wound my way through the minors. Now here we were in historic Yankee Stadium, beginning what I hoped would be a long career as their hitting coach. When you work hard in this game, and you do things the right way, and you get rewarded with a moment like this one . . . amazing!

The pinstripes, the Yankees logo on my hat, the twenty-six World Championship flags waving gently in a light breeze on flagpoles circling the top of Yankee Stadium, the buzz-rumble-roar of the fifty-five thousand people in the seats that day . . . I could go on forever, and some of you may think I have already, but I'm not quite done yet.

The number on my back, 54, will forever be associated by New York Yankees fans of a certain age with Mr. Richard Michael Gossage. That's right, for six glorious seasons (1978–1983) as the Yankees' closer, Goose Gossage wore number 54. That's the closest I'm ever going to get to Cooperstown unless I drive there, and let me tell you, it feels mighty good every time I pull on my uni top. A couple of months after Goose had been announced as 2008's sole Baseball Hall of Fame inductee, I asked him if he wanted me to change my uni number, now that he was on his way to Cooperstown. Goose said he couldn't think of anybody he'd rather see wear his number than me. I told him I'd wear it until it was retired. He said—and these were Goose's exact words—"Wear it proudly, kid."

Standing next to Donnie Mattingly, I looked up and saw Marcey in the stands in the family section. She had a huge smile on her face and was waving and blowing kisses at me. We had gone through so much together, and I knew how proud and happy she was about what we'd accomplished. My dad; his wife, Betsy; my mom; her husband, John; my grandma Jane; my brother, Tim; and his wife, Claire—they were my starting lineup of supporters that awesome day. Grandma was in tears most of the afternoon, just about overwhelmed by the fact that she was watching her grandson make his big-league debut with the New York Yankees. Dad got all choked up when he told me later, several times, how proud he was of me.

And Marcey?

What do you think?

You know when Tom Hanks says in *A League of Their Own* that "there's no crying in baseball"? Well, let me tell you that at about 1:00 on April 2, 2007, at Yankee Stadium, there was almost a whole bunch of crying right down on the first-base line, before the game even got started.

Now Coming to the Plate, Marcey Long

Opening Day 2007. Our first "real" game at Yankee Stadium— that is, our first when the batting coach of the New York Yankees was Kevin Richard Long.

The kids were in school and stayed back in Scottsdale, but everybody else in Kevin's immediate family was there.

It was a bitterly cold April day, but I was so excited I didn't even feel the wind on my face. The pregame festivities were thrilling. Kevin and I had worked so hard and gone through so much for this moment that I was simply overwhelmed with emotion.

And I wasn't the only one: I will never forget the tears trickling down Grandma Jane's face as they played the national anthem.

Now let's get back to the ball game.

Trust me, after all that pregame stuff was over and home plate umpire Gary Darling gave the signal, I was all focus and concentration. After all, I was on the clock.

We beat the Tampa Bay Devil Rays 9–5 in a game that was actually a lot closer than the final score indicated. We got off to a 2–0 lead in the first. Tampa Bay came back with a run in the second to make it 2–1. We added a third run in the fourth on a Jorge Posada homer, but in the fifth the Devil Rays scored four times to knock Carl Pavano out of the game and take a 5–3 lead. Derek Jeter tied it for us with a two-out, two-run single in the sixth. In the seventh, Alex Rodriguez singled and stole second, and Jason Giambi drove him in with what would prove to be the winning run. (Jason had 3 RBIs on the day.) We added three insurance runs in the eighth, two of them coming on a homer by Alex.

Alex had what you might call a yo-yo day. He was cheered politely during the pregame introductions, booed pretty hard after dropping a pop fly in the top half of the first and striking out on a bad pitch in the bottom half, then brought out for a curtain call by happy Yankees fans after his two-run shot in the eighth.

"It changed so much in five at bats, just like the stock market," Rodriguez said to reporters after the game. "But I'll tell you what, that curtain call made me feel really good. You just build from the positive."

And build he did: Alex went on to lead the majors in home runs (54), RBIs (156), slugging percentage (.645), and runs scored (143). Not bad after hearing a chorus of boos in your very first at bat of the year.

"Gee, Kevin," I hope somebody reading that game account will write in to ask, "did you really remember all those details about Opening Day of the 2007 season?"

"Sure," I'll answer. "I remember every swing and every hit of every guy I work with." And if you believe me, I'm going to offer you a really good deal on the Brooklyn Bridge.

No, I looked it all up. (Thank you, Google.) Once I started thinking about it, I wanted to relive every minute—every swing, every hit—of my first day as a New York Yankee.

Can you blame me?

My journey to the first-base line in Yankee Stadium that beautiful April day began three years earlier in 2004, in Columbus, Ohio. Columbus is known to the rest of the sports world as the home of the Ohio State Buckeyes, but I will always associate it with the Columbus Clippers, the Yankees' longtime AAA franchise (1979–2006) in the International League.

Much as I loved my time with the Kansas City Royals organization, I was thrilled by my change to a new uni because I felt from the get-go— no, I *knew*—that Columbus and the Yankees represented a huge opportunity for me. More money? Sure, we always needed that, but Marcey was still far and away the primary breadwinner of the family. What Columbus meant to me was that I was a giant step up the ladder to my ultimate goal: the majors.

In my three seasons with the Clippers (2004–6), I worked under two managers, Bucky Dent and Dave Miley. Every Yankees fan remembers Bucky. (So, of course, does every Red Sox fan.) Most Yankees fans haven't heard of Dave, a guy who—like me—spent his entire playing career (eight seasons, also like me) in the minors. Dave was a catcher in the Reds' organization until he hung 'em up at the end of 1987 and moved into coaching. They say that catchers are the smartest guys on the field, and based on my contact with Dave, I'd say that "they" are right. Later, he managed the Reds for one full season (2004) and parts of two others (2003, 2005). Dave currently manages our AAA team in Scranton, Pennsylvania. He does a great job there and the organization really respects him.

I tip my cap to Bucky and Dave, who were important guides in my journey to Yankee Stadium. I also learned a lot from two pitching coaches I worked with at Columbus, former Mets stopper Neil Allen and Gil Patterson, who pitched one season for the Yankees (1977). And I remember fondly a lot of laughs (and a lot of good advice) from coaches Jack Hubbard, Ty Hawkins, and Frank "Hondo" Howard. (At five-foot-eight on my tiptoes, I tried to avoid standing next to Hondo, who, at six-foot-seven and 255 pounds—his listed weight as a player; he drifted a bit north of that as a coach—is the biggest ballplayer I've ever shared a team logo with.)

Triple-A baseball is especially challenging for a hitting coach. A lot of the guys you work with have played in the majors and are crazy to do whatever it takes to get back. The others are close, so close, to taking that last big step up. My goal for all of them was to help them get more consistency, to identify and weed out bad habits—usually very little things; you don't make it up to AAA if you have major flaws—that are holding them back. At that level, I was subtracting (bad stuff) more than I was adding (new stuff). I'm proud of my contribution in helping so many Clippers fulfill their dream.

Columbus was a AAA franchise, but going over the Clippers' rosters from my three seasons there to refresh my memory for this book, I was startled by the number of position players who either played in the majors before Columbus or went on up later for at least a taste of the majors: forty! That's a lot from one team over a three-year period. (And that's not even counting the pitchers, who weren't in my department.)

The best of the forty?

That's easy—my man, Robinson Cano.

That first September call-up with the Royals in 2003, I was uncertain of what to expect. Unfortunately, I didn't get to experience the pressure and excitement of a pennant race. My good buddy Tony Peña had the boys believing in themselves and won Manager of the Year for guiding the team to an 83–79 record, good for third place in a strong AL West. But I learned a lot by the end of the month, after I'd gotten a taste of how things were done in the big leagues. My day would come, I was sure of it, but for now I was there to learn and take it all in.

Royals hitting coach Jeff Pentland made me feel right at home from Day 1. He put me to work helping with the drills, and he told me to work with the roster expansion guys just as I had in the minor leagues. Jeff and I worked great together, and he helped me a ton. I came to really admire the man, even though he had gone to Arizona State. Unlike me at U of A, Jeff spent a lot of time going to class; he had a bachelor's *and* a master's degree from ASU. He majored in something called biomechanics, which he said helped him understand the "physics of hitting." (One other thing: Jeff and my dad had gone to Grant High School together, back in Los Angeles, where they were good friends.)

That September call-up in 2003 underscored my feeling that it was only a matter of time before I'd be the hitting coach of the Kansas City Royals.

Turns out I was right about the job but wrong about the team.

My first September call-up with the Yankees in 2004 was a whole different ball game. The Yankees are always in playoff contention, and every game matters. When you're a Yankee, you're expected to win: the owners spend the most money in the majors in order to reach that goal, and Yankees fans look at the championship flags—now twenty-seven—circling the top of the grandstand and figure, hey, we need another one of those babies.

Winning is the norm in the South Bronx.

My two September call-ups with the Yankees (I went up again in 2005) played a critical role in my understanding of what it takes to be a New York Yankee. I got a crash course in New York's streets and subways and packed restaurants. I saw more TV cameras and reporters with mikes and notebooks than I'd encountered in my entire eighteen seasons in the minors. I had the honor and privilege of observing up close how players and coaches and the manager of the most successful team in baseball history interact in a pennant race, and, yes, I had a great seat for the historic showdown between the Yankees and the Red Sox in the 2004 ALCS.

Time out! That last bit's not true. I *felt* like I had a great seat for that seven-game heartbreaker for Yankees fans, because I felt so much like I was a part of the team. But coaches called up when rosters expand aren't allowed to sit in the dugout during games. No numbers on our backs, either; we had to wear warm-up jackets on the field before games. And before the first pitch, we had to leave the field and the dugout and go back into the clubhouse, where we'd watch the game TV in the players' lounge.

Hey, all that was okay by me. I was like, *Look, dude, this is the clubhouse of the* New York Yankees. *Don't pinch yourself or you might wake up.* And I'd kick back and follow every pitch.

Now Coming to the Plate, Marcey Long

My first-ever visit to New York City came when Kevin was called up in September 2004, and Jaron, my girlfriend Allison Baile, and I joined him there for a long weekend. We were tourists to the max: Central Park, the Empire State Building, Rockefeller Center, and, of course, three games at Yankee Stadium. That's when I started dreaming and praying that someday Kevin would wear pinstripes full-time, and we would call New York City home, at least during the baseball season.

For the playoffs against the Red Sox that year, I met Kev in Boston alone. October 15 is my birthday, and that night the game was rained out. The coaches' wives didn't even leave the hotel because of the weather. So when the guys returned after the game was officially called, Kevin and I went out to dinner. When we got back to our hotel room, there were a few

birthday presents waiting for me: flowers from our daughter,
Britney, and a nice bottle of champagne from one of my girl-
friends. Kev asked, "What's all this stuff?"

"Babe," I broke the news to him gently, "it's my birthday."
Poor guy! He had other things on his mind.

In 2005, I was pleasantly surprised when the Yankees got a clear-
ance from MLB for the September call-up coaches to be in the dugout.
Still no uni number, but I was right there on the bench as we finished
90–72 to win the AL East. (I'd rather not talk about our loss to the Angels in the AL Division Series.)

Watching September–October baseball games on TV, as I had the
year before, is fine, but it doesn't hold a candle to watching them from
the dugout.

Being part of those playoff runs in 2004 and 2005 would prove invaluable a couple of years later in my preparation for the 2007 and 2009
playoffs. Even though I didn't have a number on my back—yet—I'd
been devastated in 2004 when we lost a 3–0 lead in the ALCS to
the Red Sox and they eventually went on to win the World Series.
As tough as that was to swallow, the fresh, raw memory of it was also
motivation for me. I was determined to help the Yankees get over the
disappointment and find their way back to the World Series, where
we belonged.

Don Mattingly was unbelievably great to me during those two Septembers (and in spring training, as well). The guy may be a big name
in Yankees history, but he most certainly doesn't have a big head to
go with it. He's the most humble "star" you'd ever want to meet. He
showed me the ropes, and he listened patiently when I'd expound my
theories. Not once did he talk down to me or make me feel unwanted.

What I'm getting at is that Donnie didn't just tolerate me around the cage. He'd ask me questions, solicit my opinions, and go back and forth with me if we didn't have exactly the same take on something. He wasn't just going through the motions. With another kind of guy, I could have been on pins and needles or felt shut out the whole time on those September call-ups and spring training encounters. Instead, Donnie made me feel like I was part of the team. As Jeff Pentland had done in 2002 and 2003 in KC, Donnie let me pitch in and work with all the roster expansion guys. His theory was that if I could help them in any way, then why not let me? He also knew that I'd worked with many of these guys in Columbus, and that I probably understood their swings better than anybody.

(Mattingly, of course, took over as manager of the Dodgers after the 2010 season. Naturally, I wish him well and all success—unless, of course, we should come up against each other some October.)

As for "replacing" Don Mattingly as Yankees hitting coach, that idea wasn't a weight around my neck because I never gave it a thought. How do you replace a legend? You don't. Get caught up in that sort of thinking and you're setting yourself up to fail. The Yankees hired me for what they thought *I* could bring to the team, period. My biggest booster— outside of Marcey, of course—was none other than Donnie himself. He was very excited for me, and he expressed complete confidence that I could do the job. From my first day on the job, he and Joe Torre really let me do my thing.

That underscored the inner confidence that I had in myself.

I believed in my heart that I was ready.

I hit the ground running.

7 | GETTING DOWN TO BUSINESS

On October 30, 2006, the Yankees announced that Don Mattingly had been promoted to bench coach and that yours truly had been signed as their new batting coach.

As you can imagine, the next couple of days around our house in Phoenix were a blur of "I can't believe it!" and "Kev, you really did it!" and "No, babe, *we* did it!" and "When do we get to move to New York, Dad?" I heard from all my family, a lot of old friends from high school, and a bunch of guys I'd played with in the KC organization. Several Yankees called to congratulate me and welcome me aboard. All that felt good, really good.

But, hey, I had a job to do! All the celebrating was great, and believe me, we did a bunch of it, but I needed to get to *work*.

My first move was to get video on each of our players so I could start getting to know their swings. About all I could think of was how much homework I had to do before spring training camp opened. By Thanksgiving I'd talked at least once with most of the team.

Thrilled? Excited? Raring to go? Sure, all of the above. And maybe a little bit scared? Funny, no, not really. As I reflect back, that surprises me a little. Part of my not being scared, I know, had to do with my confidence in my own ability and my understanding of the art of hitting. And part of it, of course, was not knowing how much I *didn't* know yet about coping with the pressures of performing on the major-league level.

Good thing, too. You know what they say—ignorance is bliss. Had I known how much I didn't know, I'd have freaked out.

I spent my first off-season as a Yankee—the 153 days between October 30, 2006, and trotting out to the first-base line in Yankee Stadium on April 2, 2007—playing some fast and furious catch-up ball.

Tick-tock . . . tick-tock . . . tick-tock . . .

So much to do, so little time. I tried my best to be a good husband and father during this period, but I know that I didn't give Marcey and the kids the attention they deserved. The love was there, though, strong as ever, and I knew they were behind me 110 percent. We came out the other end of that challenging time stronger than ever as a family.

The first assignment I gave myself was to establish personal contact with every single one of the players I'd be working with come spring training. To me, this was absolutely essential. I didn't want to march into the clubhouse at the Yankees' spring training complex in Tampa in February and say, "Hi, guys, we've never talked, but my name's Kevin Long, and I'm your new hitting coach. Let's get to work."

Maybe I couldn't meet every guy personally during that first off-season, and getting to know each other would take time. But if I couldn't actually get to know a guy, I could get to know his swing. Looking back, it seems like I spent most of my waking hours that first off-season sitting in front of a TV monitor. Every day I watched hours and hours of video, analyzing the swings of my new bosses. That's right, bosses: I was working for them was the way I saw it. (Still do.) I wanted to develop a mental image of what they looked like when they were going good and what they looked like when they were struggling.

After all, my biggest challenge was going to be building relationships and earning trust. To do that, I'd have to learn their swings inside out, and I couldn't afford to wait to see them in person to get started.

Cue the video.

The first Yankee I worked with on a one-to-one basis was one of the highest-profile players on the team.

Alex Rodriguez called right after my news became public, congratulated me, and asked me if there was a time during the off-season that we could get together and start swinging the bat. Well, uh, sure, I said. I admit to being practically tongue-tied.

For one thing, in the minors a coach doesn't spend time with his players during the off-season. Because of all the movement up and down (up's better), you don't really know who your guys are going to be until the next season starts. And even if you did, you couldn't afford to fly back and forth across the country on a coach's salary to work with your players.

"Fine, Alex. Just name a time and a place that works for you, and I'll be there."

Alex asked me if I'd seen him swing much, and I said, yes, I had—not much in game action, I told him, only during my September call-ups in 2004 and 2005. But I had studied his swing in spring training the previous March in Tampa and in a few video clips. He asked me if I thought it could get better and more consistent. I hemmed and hawed a little, but my answer was yes, I thought there were a couple of things that I thought he might want to consider trying. I threw out a couple of ideas, and he got excited. I mean, the man was ready to get started the day before yesterday.

Could I possibly come down to Miami and work with him? You bet, I said, and in early December I hopped on a plane to Miami. That first trip we mostly talked concepts and got to know each other. I went again in late January, a month before spring training began, and we spent most of the time in the cage. Since then working with Alex for a few days has been the keystone of my off-season routine.

Where do you start with a guy with two MVP awards, ten All-Star Game appearances, 464 homers, and a BA well north of .300 in the eleven seasons he played before you showed up as his new hitting coach? Good question, one I spent that entire first flight from Phoenix to Miami rolling around in my head. I was slightly nervous. Okay, more than slightly. After all, I was just about to begin my first year in the big leagues after eighteen straight seasons in the minors. Alex had already put up Hall of Fame numbers. What a huge relief when I met him and our talk about ideas went great: Alex showed he was open and willing to experiment.

The bottom line: A-Rod's swing was one the best in baseball before he ever met me, and it would continue to be so, with or without K-Long. My challenge wasn't to remake it but simply to make it more consistent.

To achieve that goal, I told Alex, I wanted to add by subtracting. Not give him a whole bunch of new things to do, but to eliminate or rein in a few things that occasionally crept into his swing and robbed him of the consistency he was after. Alex hadn't been happy with his 2006 season when he'd hit "only" .290, with 35 HRs and 121 RBIs. A guy with numbers like that, you'd think he would kick back and play golf or go skiing or something until spring training. Not Alexander Emmanuel "A-Rod" Rodriguez, whose drive, combined with his amazing talent, is what makes him such a great baseball player. His home-run total had been his lowest in ten years, and he thought he could do better.

After about a gazillion hours screening video of his swing before getting in that plane and flying south, so did I.

My plan called for Alex to focus on three mechanical fundamentals. The first was to minimize and shorten the height of his leg kick. The second was to get him to stay on his back side and use the lower half of his body more. The third was to take away excess forward movement that occasionally crept into his swing.

LEG KICK

This was going to take some work. A leg kick with a forward stride on his front side had always been Alex's trigger or timing mechanism for his swing. My goal wasn't to take this away from him, but to get him to control it better and to help him be on time with it.

To control the height of his leg kick and the distance gained with it, I would first have to demonstrate to him what was happening and make him aware of it. I had him show me the ideal contact point in his swing. Then I had him pick up his front leg above his belt while balancing on his back leg, like a drum major preparing to strut down the field. When he had his leg in the air in this exaggerated pose, I asked him if that was close to the contact point or extremely far from it.

The answer was a no-brainer: it was a mile away from where he needed to be at contact. Our goal was simply to get closer to the hitting position, with smaller movements. In other words, keep the leg kick, but lower the height of it and eliminate moving toward the pitcher.

To get there, I asked Alex to widen his base and focus on picking up his leg and setting his foot down in the same spot. Some players, you make a suggestion like that, and they nod, okay, sure, I got it—but they don't. Their muscles and minds are so programmed to doing things a certain way that they aren't able to make the physical adjustment, at least not at first.

Not Alex. He was able to do it immediately. He widened his base, got flexion in his legs, and made a subtle up-and-down move with his front leg. Not a big change to the naked eye, but very big in our world. Alex now had a modified leg kick that we thought would help get him into a better position to react to the baseball.

BACK SIDE AND LOWER HALF

Now that we had his base set better and had reduced his leg kick, I asked Alex to focus on keeping his back foot in place and driving his back knee down and through during the swing. In recent years, he had sometimes let his back foot slide forward and not always driven into his core and legs properly. Obviously, it didn't happen all the time, but when it did, it robbed him of power and caused him to be way out ahead on off-speed pitches or late on fastballs. (How did I know this? Trust me, I watched a *lot* of film of Mr. Rodriguez before I made that second trip down to Miami.)

Alex had always been very explosive and strong—just check his numbers since 1996, his first full season in the majors—but we both felt like his swing could be better if he stayed centered and didn't try to go and get the ball.

This actually turned out to be a very easy adjustment for him.

DECREASE FORWARD MOVEMENT IN THE SWING

Everybody I know teaches staying tight and compact to the baseball. Any hitting coach who doesn't ought to consider moving into another sport. The idea: decrease forward movement of the body so as not to create extra distance to the ball.

Stay back and centered!

Don't reach!

That's the intended consequence of shortening the leg kick and making better use of the lower half. Many times you'll see Alex hold his position at the end of his swing, especially on home runs. He's not posing for a photo op, and he's certainly not trying to show up the pitcher. He's trying to strengthen the muscle memory of what he's just done, the technical term for which is "back-leggin' shit!"

(Coaches in Pee Wee Baseball may want to come up with another term for that. Not because the kids won't get the concept; they will. But some Pee Wee parents may give you a little grief.)

Something worked, because in 2007, our first season working together, Alex hit 54 homers, drove in 156 runs, batted .314, and won his third MVP award.

The man is definitely a quick study.

Since we started working together that winter of 2006, Alex has maintained solid swing mechanics that, combined with his extraordinary natural ability, have produced some mighty fine results. (Again, let me restate the obvious: Alex was a great hitter way before he knew me. We were just looking at ways to keep him in that groove.) A few small issues creep in now and again, but nothing major, nothing he and I can't work out in a short period of time.

You want a dream student of hitting?

Take a look at the guy in the pinstripes with number 13 on his back.

Johnny Damon and I had been roommates in Wichita in 1995 when we were both with the Kansas City organization. Unlike some roommates, we became and stayed good friends. In fact, J.D.'s one of my best friends in baseball. But now, in 2007, we had a whole different relationship to deal with. Johnny was just beginning his second season with New York, and I was his new hitting coach.

Johnny was already a huge favorite among Yankees fans when I showed up. That happens when you hit for power, steal bases, and hustle like a demon while playing center field in the House That Ruth Built. I know him as one of the best character guys in baseball, a true gamer, someone I respect a great deal.

J.D. plays the game right, he knows the game inside out, and he can really hit good pitching. Check out his lifetime .347 BA against Roy Halladay, one of the best pitchers in the game. Johnny may be one of the true free spirits in the game today, but he really bears down against the best.

One of my biggest moments as a coach that first year in 2007 came on May 30 after we'd beaten the Blue Jays in Toronto. J.D. called me out of the coaches' room and told me he wanted me to have something. He got choked up as he told me that he knew how hard I had worked to get to the big leagues, and he handed me a baseball—the one he'd pounded for his two thousandth hit that night.

Talk about losing it! To this day, going on four years later, I tear up just thinking about him giving me that ball.

His swing? Oh, sure, we worked on it some. J.D. has a very unorthodox swing, but he's been very successful with it, so we didn't do any dramatic overhauls. (Don't fix it if it ain't broke!) There were just a few things that I wanted to be sure we stayed on top of. We always talked about his bat staying flat through the zone and staying into his legs—that is, using them throughout the swing, not coming up and out as he moved the bat to the ball. And, of course, there's J.D. and "pulling."

Johnny Damon is the only player I've ever coached who, when he's consciously trying to pull the ball, becomes a better hitter. I'm a huge believer in consciously trying to stay in the gaps and the middle of the field when hitting. To try and hook around the ball on purpose so you can pull it is just not a sane idea, because it leaves you vulnerable to breaking pitches and creates length in your swing. But for J.D., thinking "pull" gets him started and on time. All that movement you see takes a while to get him to the hitting position, so the more he consciously tries to pull, the more ready he is to hit.

Our relationship when we were with the Yankees together from 2007 through 2009 was a little strange. We'd been players on the same team in the minors, roomies for goodness' sake, now here I was his coach, his *hitting instructor,* me never having made the majors, and him having been a star on four teams. And even though we were good friends, we couldn't go out together and drink beers on nights after a win, the way we had back in Wichita. Though Johnny and I did go out together on occasion, we never crossed the (invisible) line. As I said, a little strange.

(By the way, that old, unwritten rule saying that players and coaches shouldn't hang out together away from the ballpark has relaxed a lot in recent years. Not so long ago, Johnny and I—player and coach—wouldn't have hung out together at all. Today, players and coaches will often go out to eat after a game or occasionally grab a cold beverage. Personally, I think that's a good thing. I believe it helps bring a team together and makes it a stronger unit. Nowadays, a big age gap between player and coach is more likely to inhibit socializing than some outmoded "code.")

In 2009, J.D. was one of the keys to our championship season. Batting second between Jeet (Derek Jeter)and Tex (Mark Teixeira), Johnny hit .282, tied his career high with 24 home runs, drove in 82 runs, stole 12 bases, scored 107 runs, and led the league in hustle. J.D.'s 107 runs scored put him in a tie with Jeet for fourth place in the American League. Tex and Robbie (Robinson Cano) weren't far behind, by the way; at 103, they tied with two other guys for sixth place. No wonder we were such a run-scoring machine in 2009! We led the league in runs scored by 32, and those four guys alone accounted for 46 percent of our 915 total!

So how come the Yankees let J.D. walk as a free agent and sign with the Tigers? Maybe money: he'd just finished a four-year deal at $13 million per. Maybe age: Johnny turned thirty-six four days before he became a free agent. Maybe a combination of the two, or maybe . . . hey, wait a minute, this isn't my department.

I do know this: Yankees fans miss him, and so do I.

J.D., I wish you all success, old buddy.

Except, of course, when you and the Rays pay a visit to the Stadium or we come down to see you in Tampa in 2011.

8 | WORK, WORK, WORK— AND THEN WORK SOME MORE

The one thing a hitting coach absolutely, positively must have—and this is something I concluded in the first month of my first season on the job with the Kansas City organization in 1997—is a willingness to learn something new every day.

Every single day.

A good hitting coach must be an absolute leech for anything that will help him make his players better hitters. And if he picks up a tiny little something that goes against what he thinks he knows? He's got to be open and willing to give it a try. Baseball is an old game, and in the kind of world we live in, it sometimes feels like it's one of the few things that is constant, unchanging. But that kind of feeling is a trap for a hitting coach. It means he no longer thinks it's important to learn new ways of looking at things or to make new adjustments that suit a particular player. That sort of resistance to change will do you in for sure.

Never, *ever* since I got into the coaching side of the game have I thought I was done learning about how to hit a baseball. I believe in my heart and soul and head that I need to keep on learning if I'm going to be any good at teaching. If I ever get to a point where I think there's nothing new I can learn about the game, I'll know that it's time to hang up my spikes for good and go find a day job.

Since day one of coaching, my goal has always been for my hitters to maximize their potential. In order to achieve this goal you must have a comprehensive plan.

The plan was to screen and utilize our video library, work and develop hitting routines for all my players, and get them to understand their swings. The process was going to take time, but I knew it would get done.

I may have been a rookie in 2007, but I was going to be the most thorough hitting coach in baseball. Don't get me wrong. Other guys with my job know a lot about hitting. Others had been terrific hitters in the big leagues themselves. But nobody, nobody was going to put forth more effort than myself.

Look, I had to be. I was a rookie, remember? And I had a lot to prove.

No other hitting coach in the majors approaches his job as methodically as I do. Nobody watches as much film as I do. Nobody prepares detailed game plans and pitcher charts the way I do. I'm not saying I'm better at what I do than the other guys in the big leagues who hold the same job title. I simply go at it differently. It's just my personality, I guess. I don't want to leave a stone unturned. I want to dot every "i" and cross every "t," because I feel like if I lose the respect of one guy, I could be on the slippery slope to losing my job. Crazy? Obsessive? Maybe a little. But that's how I do things.

This may sound a little wacko, but I don't ever want to be *comfortable* when I'm working. My feeling is that the more comfortable you get, the more you let your guard down, and that's when you slip up and lose your edge. I want to feel like I could get fired tomorrow if I am not absolutely, 100 percent on top of my game. I need that feeling if I'm going to do my job right. Can't slide by on what I did yesterday. Got to work harder today so tomorrow will be even better. Rest on my laurels? Sure, why not—when I retire.

Know what? I think that's a pretty good attitude to have no matter what your field.

Some guys are always talking themselves up to be sure you understand how smart they are. You know the kind of guys I'm talking about. You run into them in every walk of life. And if you're like me, you start looking around for the nearest exit. I try to keep to myself. I don't like to preach or carry on about what I think I know. I let my work speak for itself.

Work.

That's the most important word in my professional vocabulary.

I promise my players, I promise the guys I teach at clinics during the off-season, I promise the New York Yankees that I will not be outworked. Repeat: *I . . . will . . . not . . . be . . . outworked.*

And then I prove it to them.

A lazy coach, especially a lazy hitting coach, won't be around long. You better be prepared to work your butt off, because if you don't, if you're the least bit lackadaisical, it'll come back to bite you in the ass. You have to be really and truly tireless, because there are so many little things to monitor and to work on with every position player on the roster.

And not only do you have to work hard yourself, you have to convince your players to work hard, too.

Hey, I'm Not the Only One

What's a guy who never made it to the big leagues doing with a job title currently held by household names like Don Mattingly, Dwayne Murphy, Don Baylor, and Mark McGwire? For that answer, you'll have to speak to Joe Girardi and Brian Cashman. But I can tell you this: I'm not the only guy in the majors who never got out of the minors. The following names in boldface form a small but cocky band of brothers who know we got where we are today because of our teaching skills, not our name recognition or ML résumés.

American League, 2010

Team	Hitting Coach
Orioles	Terry Crowley
Red Sox	Dave Magadan
White Sox	Greg Walker
Indians	Jon Nunnally
Tigers	Lloyd McClendon
Royals	Kevin Seitzer
Angels	Mickey Hatcher
Twins	**Joe Vavra**
Yankees	**Kevin Long**
A's	**Jim Skaalen**
Mariners	Alan Cockrell
Rays	**Derek Shelton**
Rangers	Clint Hurdle
Blue Jays	Dwayne Murphy

National League, 2010

Team	Hitting Coach
Diamondbacks	Jack Howell
Braves	Terry Pendleton
Cubs	**Rudy Jaramillo**
Reds	Brook Jacoby
Rockies	Don Baylor
Marlins	Jim Presley
Astros	Sean Berry
Dodgers	Don Mattingly
Brewers	Dale Sveum
Mets	Howard Johnson
Phillies	Milt Thompson
Pirates	**Don Long**

Padres	Randy Ready
Giants	Hensley Meulens
Cardinals	Mark McGwire
Nationals	**Rick Eckstein**

After the season's over, I do some clinics, I touch base at least once with each of my guys, and I get reacquainted with my golf clubs, but I spend most of November and December putting in quality time with Marcey and my family.

("Hi, babe. Remember me? I'm Kevin . . .")

By early January, though, almost two months before position players report to spring training, I'm back in work mode. That's when I make my annual trip down to Miami to spend a few days with Alex. We talk about hitting. I ask him what things he thinks need some work. I volunteer a couple of notions of my own. Then we head out to his batting cage adjacent to his gorgeous house in Coral Gables. For readers in two-thirds of the country, four or five days in Florida in the first two weeks of January doesn't sound exactly like hard labor, and it's not. But that has less to do with the weather—hey, I live in Scottsdale; the winter weather's pretty nice there, too—than the fact that I'm doing something I really love.

Besides working with any Yankee who wants to see me, I do a lot of day and weekend clinics over the winter—"Have Bat, Will Travel" ought to be my motto, Marcey says. My favorite off-season gig for the past few years has been the Pro-Ball Baseball Clinic at the San Diego Padres' spring training facility in Peoria, Arizona. Never heard of it? If you're a serious amateur ballplayer, no matter what your age, it's time you do.

The Pro-Ball Baseball Clinic is the brainchild of a doctor turned actor turned TV-ad star named John Rubinow. (He's one of the guys in the TV ad extolling the virtues of Levitra, the magic erectile dysfunction pill.) The first Pro-Ball Clinic was in 2002. Now there are two, the Fundamentals Clinic in January and an Advanced Skills Clinic in December, and John hopes to add a Fathers-Sons Clinic in 2012. In 2010, the Fundamentals Clinic topped out at seventy-two campers, a big enough jump from the year before that at the last minute John had to bring in some additional coaches from the greater Phoenix area to help with the teaching load. I think it's a good deal—$2,795 for a long weekend, not counting travel—because of the quality of the instruction offered. The Fundamentals Clinic, the one I'm most familiar with, attracts a bunch of guys ranging in age (mostly) from their midthirties to midfifties, with a couple of gents on the far side of sixty. Plus there's one regular in his early seventies who looks like he's in his early sixties and swings a bat like he's in his early forties. In 2010, he was accompanied by his son and two grandsons.

So right about now you're probably thinking ho-hum, just another fantasy camp, where a bunch of grown-up fans who've never quite grown up put on the unis of their favorite teams, play a couple of sloppy games a day, and hang out at the bar at night with a couple of medium-well-known ex-ballplayers.

No.

Not even close.

See, the Pro-Ball Baseball Clinic is a *work* camp. No team uniforms; campers bring their own. Games? Yes, but they're really a sidelight. Players spend the bulk of each day on basic hitting, fielding, and pitching skills under the guidance of what, if I do say so myself, is a blue-ribbon faculty.

My fellow instructors on the hitting side in 2010 included Jim Presley (Orioles hitting coach), Brook Jacoby (Reds), cranky, funny Tony Muser (minor-league hitting coordinator for the Padres and former manager of the Royals, 1997–2002), Lee Tinsley (roving outfield/baserunning instructor for the Cubs), Bob Apodaca (Rockies pitching coach), Mike Butcher (Angels pitching coach), Rob Picciolo (fifteen years as the Angels' infield coach), Orv Franchuk (field manager for the Edmonton Capitals in the Independent League), Ty Van Burkleo (roving hitting instructor for the Astros), and Glenn Shurlock (bullpen/catching coach, Diamondbacks). Glenn also functions as Pro-Ball's manager. Oh, and yours truly.

For the players, Pro-Ball is a lot of fun, but that's not the main reason they're there. They come to improve their basic baseball skills so they can get the most out of the fifty, sixty, one hundred, *or more* games they play every year in the Men's Senior Baseball League (MSBL)/Men's Adult Baseball League (MABL). The MSBL/MABL is a national organization with nearly fifty thousand members and thirty-two hundred teams in 325 localities across the country. (Did you know that? Neither did I until I worked my first Pro-Ball clinic.)

So far, I've taught at five Pro-Ball clinics. I hope I keep on getting invited back. Why? Well, it's a winter payday, and Marcey and I spent so many years struggling to make ends meet that it's almost second nature for us to pick up part-time gigs between seasons. Plus the Padres spring training camp is only a short commute from my house in Scottsdale; I already spend so much of the year away from home that I try to minimize my travel during the off-season. (I said "try." Somehow I end up doing something somewhere—a clinic here, another there— just about every weekend.)

But mainly I continue to teach at John's Pro-Ball Baseball Clinic because I really like his concept. (This year—2011—I'm going to have to skip Fundamentals in January, but I'll be working at Advanced Skills in December.) The thing I find most attractive about the Pro-Ball clinics, the thing that keeps me coming back, is that the guys who come to it are so damned dedicated to getting better. They come to *work*.

To me, that's like dragging catnip in front of a cat.

"Okay, let's get started. Step up to the plate . . ."

My first priority, of course, is to the Yankees. Every winter I'll get a call from one Yankee or another asking if I would mind coming around to work with him on a few things. *Mind?* Man, I love it when one of my guys calls me up and asks if we can get together to work on a thing or two.

Yo! My place or yours?

In early January 2010, just a couple of months after we won the World Championship, I flew over to Miami for my customary winter drills with Alex. Tex was in town to watch his alma mater, Georgia Tech, play Iowa in the Orange Bowl. He hung around for a few days before the game (Hawkeyes 24, Yellow Jackets 14), and he and Alex worked out together (weights and running).

Think about that for a minute. These guys were coming off monster seasons (Tex: 39, 122, .292; Alex: 30, 100, .286), we were world champions, and *still* they wanted to get together just after New Year's Day to "work on a few things." Tex doesn't like to start hitting until a little closer to spring training, but Alex spent some quality time in the cage. I tell you, it was really great to get together with those guys and talk about the 2009 season and just hang out. Jorge Posada and his family had moved to Miami that off-season, which made it convenient for Jorge and me to have lunch and catch up on Yankees off-season news.

For ballplayers and coaches and managers, the days positively fly by between the last out of the season and those words that thrill baseball fans all over the country: "Pitchers and Catchers," as in, "Pitchers and catchers report this weekend." The 162-game season, with all the travel and the pressure and the intensity, can grind a body down. And if you're good enough and lucky enough to tack on playoffs and—if you're *really* good and *really* lucky—the World Series, you get an idea of what the old saying "It's a long season" really means.

So when a player shows me he wants to devote a piece of his precious off-season to working with me on something, it thrills me, it really does. It shows me how much he cares, how much he respects what I have to offer, and how much he's committed to putting in the work needed to be the best ballplayer he can possibly be.

The off-season following the 2009 season was especially short because the Yankees did what we're always supposed to do, win the World Series. You might think all the guys would have pretty much shut down between November 5, the day after we won our twenty-seventh World Championship, and February 23, when position players reported to the Yankees' spring training complex in Tampa. That would be perfectly understandable.

Think again.

Back in the good old days, from what I've read and been told by old-timers, a lot of big-league ballplayers spent the long off-season putting on beer bellies, knowing they'd have plenty of time during spring training to take them off. (Or not.)

But for today's major leaguers, the off-season ends shortly after the New Year's Day bowl games (but before the Super Bowl), when they start cranking it up. Most guys start working out that first week of January, sometimes alone, but often with other ballplayers who live nearby. Guys from other teams as well as their own? Sure. After all, in the off-season all big leaguers share a single goal: to keep on being big leaguers.

Some restrict these preseason workouts to cardio and strength drills; others fold in a little cage time. My point is that just about every player in major-league baseball—the minors, too—is working hard getting ready for the next season a good two months before it starts. They come to camp fit and raring to go.

Each off-season presents new challenges for me.

Let me tell you about just three other Yankees I worked with during the off-season after the 2009 World Championship. I guess you could say they were my top three "winter projects": Nick Swisher, Nick Johnson, and Curtis Granderson.

Nick Swisher started working on his swing with me in Phoenix, near my home in Scottsdale, in early December. Later that month I spent three intense days with Nick Johnson, who came to us after signing a free-agent contract. And in early February, Curtis Granderson, who came over to us from the Tigers in a three-team trade, visited me in Scottsdale. Those three guys focused their attention on three different areas, but they demonstrated one trait in common: an understanding of the value of work.

NICK SWISHER

Boy, do Yankees fans love Swish, especially his buddies in the right-field bleachers. Good reason, too: he's a legitimately nice guy who loves the back-and-forth with fans. Swish is so outgoing, so laid-back, that you might guess he'd have a casual attitude toward the game. Not so. Swish is a worker, a *hard* worker. He puts in good, quality time in the cage, and he's open to new ideas and suggestions.

Truth is, he's a hitting coach's dream come true.

In 2008, when he was with the White Sox, Swish hit .219 with 24 homers and 69 RBIs, and he had 82 walks and 135 strikeouts. In 2009, his first season with the Yankees, we got him up to .249-29-82, with 107 walks and 126 strikeouts. Now the improvement in the power numbers has a lot to do with the change in teams and ballparks: the better the team, the more chances for RBIs. And of course there's the friendly right-field porch in Yankee Stadium (314 feet down the line) that's been putting smiles on the faces of left-handed power hitters since the day it opened in 1923.

Speaking of the Stadium, it's undergone a couple of major face-lifts over the years. The most recent and most extensive change was completed just in time for the opening of the 2009 season. In my view, the great thing about the new Yankee Stadium is that the outfield dimensions are exactly the same as in the old one. Baseball is a game of tradition and history, but new stadiums built in the last quarter of a century have paid no mind to that. The only three ballparks in the majors that would be recognizable to a baseball fan from fifty years ago are Wrigley Field, Fenway Park, and, I'm proud to say, Yankee Stadium.

Now, back to Swish. What I like when I look at his numbers in 2008 and 2009 is the increase in walks and the decrease—only a small drop, but a drop nonetheless—in his strikeouts. My goal for Swish going into 2010 was for him to boost his average to around .280. I knew that would be a terrific measure of his development as a hitter. It would take real focus and discipline at the plate, and a lot of hard work in the cage to make sure he nipped every wannabe bad habit in the bud, but I thought he was up to the challenge.

You know what? I blew it. I set the bar too low. In 2010, Swish hit 29 home runs, drove in 89 runs—and batted .288.

NICK JOHNSON

My initial goal with both Nick Johnson and Curtis Granderson prior to the beginning of the 2010 season was to get acquainted with their swings and begin building relationships with them. The sessions with both guys went very well; I learned a lot. That was important. With new guys especially, but also with veterans, I have to be constantly learning if I'm going to be a worthwhile teacher.

Johnson was to fill the DH role vacated by the departure of Hideki Matsui to the Angels after the 2009 season. Nick's an on-base machine; he went into his first year as a Yankee with a .402 lifetime OBP, ninth best among active major leaguers. (He had only 98 plate appearances in 2010 because of an injury, so his .388 OBP doesn't mean he's lost his great eye at the plate.) But I wondered if we could keep that strength and boost a couple of others. Looking at Nick's video tracks, I spotted a couple of things going on with the lower half of his body that I thought needed some work. When Nick arrived at my house, we talked for a while and then headed to my buddy Andy Goulder's indoor cage. Andy and his wife, Charlie, have a beautiful house nearby, but what makes it even better is the cage that sits inside their gymnasium. I can't thank the Goulders enough for all their generosity in letting me use the cage over the past ten years.

Nick and I hit off the tee, did a lot of front toss, and spent a long time on one of my personal favorites, the net drill, which emphasizes staying tight to your core and inside the ball.

The main thing I picked up from our work together was that Nick needed to focus on using his back leg more efficiently. Nick's back leg tended to slide back and collapse, causing him to lose power and explosiveness to the ball. I explained that I thought he needed to keep his back foot in place and have it turn in sync with his hands. That would get his lower body more involved in the swing, which in turn would put him in better position to drive inside pitches. I explained to Nick what I thought the benefits would be to him: an increase in power and a better batting average, which in turn would boost his runs scored and RBIs.

Look, Nick's already been there, done that: he had 23 homers to go with a .290 batting average for the Nationals in 2006. I just wanted him to gain more consistency and maximize his potential.

To my surprise, Nick was very quick to pick up the things I talked to him about, and he liked the feel of the changes right out of the box. I say "surprise" not because I thought Nick was going to be a slow learner or anything. It's just that he'd never worked with me, and guys who've reached the big-league level are resistant to changing their swing. Perfectly understandable. After all, they'd made it to the majors with a certain swing, and all of a sudden here comes some coach they've never even met before wanting them to try something different.

My prediction to myself at the time was that Nick would hit around .300 with at least 25 homers for us in 2010. The year before, Nick hit .291 for the Nationals and the Marlins, so my "around .300" forecast wasn't exactly daring. But he had only 8 homers, so my crystal-balling him for "at least 25" was a pretty big leap. I thought he could do it, though, if he made the adjustments we worked on over the winter on the lower half of his body at the plate.

By the way, my preseason prediction was to myself *only*. I'd never, ever share concrete projections like that with a player. It would only put more pressure on him, which in the process might throw some other part of his swing off-kilter. Remember, the head—what goes on inside it—is the single most important part of a baseball player's swing.

We never got to find out whether I was on the money or way off. Nick hurt his wrist swinging in May after just twenty-four games, had surgery to repair it, and missed the rest of the season. So we won't really know until 2011 whether the things Nick and I worked on back before the 2010 season began are going to do the trick. And we'll have to see if any lingering consequences of his serious injury will require us to make other adjustments.

CURTIS GRANDERSON

The Yankees acquired Curtis from the Tigers after the 2009 season to fill the big hole left in the lineup by the departure of Johnny Damon. Johnny, of course, was signed by the Tigers to fill the vacancy left by the departure of . . . Curtis Granderson.

(After the 2010 season, the Tampa Bay Rays signed my old Wichita roomie to a one-year free agent deal. They also signed Manny Ramirez. Those two guys beef up an already strong lineup that finished third in the AL last year with 802 runs. We finished first with 859, but I have a gut feeling that those guys down in Florida will be breathing down our necks all season.)

The big issue with Grandy was his lack of production against left-handed pitching. Matter of fact, that was the *only* issue with Grandy. He normally kills right-handers, but has a well-documented history of not producing against lefties. In 2009, he hit .183 against left-handers. That's no typo: *.183*. And it was no fluke, either. Fold in the two preceding seasons and his combined BA against southpaws was a rousing .202. That helplessness against lefties explained why all but two of his thirty home runs in 2009 came off right-handers. And he'd be facing more lefties in Yankee Stadium than he ever did in Tiger Stadium.

I could go on, but you get the picture, and it wasn't a pretty one.

Shortly after we signed Grandy, I went straight to our video archives for 2007–2008–2009 and started searching for clues. After looking at a lot of feeble swings—I only screened his at bats against lefties—I developed a preliminary game plan:

1. Move him closer to the plate.
2. Help him curb his upper body tilt.
3. Convince him to keep his head behind the ball and not let it travel forward.

That was *my* game plan. My next job was to persuade Grandy to make it *his* game plan.

So in February, when Grandy came out to the desert to visit me, we wasted no time going after it. He and his agent, Matt Brown, flew into Phoenix, and we drove straight to nearby Pinnacle High School, my de facto off-season office, and we started hitting.

We started with front flips—an underhand-toss drill that helps me see all the components of a guy's swing—and I just watched him for about twenty swings. As he swung and got loose, I really liked a lot of what I saw with his swing, and I told him so. But, and this was where I needed to be both precise and positive, I explained to him that I had watched all his video against left-handed pitching, and that I'd seen a few things that troubled me, and that I had a few thoughts I wanted to share with him. He was very receptive and immediately took the information and began to work on my game plan: he moved closer to the plate; he focused hard on staying upright and not tilting his torso; and he worked consciously to keep his head behind the ball.

So far, so good, but as I told him, for a while it would be easy to fall back into old habits. I told him that I would have my eyes on him on every pitch—in BP, in exhibition games, and once the season began. Every single time I see even one tiny deviation from what we both agree you want to do, I told him, I'm going to tell you directly. No mincing words. Changing old habits is tough, really tough, and I told him it would be an uphill battle until he got them changed. A month later, in spring training, we went over his game plan on a daily basis, and he started working.

Grandy is a terrific kid, very receptive and very eager to get better, and he had clearly internalized his game plan and worked diligently to implement it once we got to Tampa last spring. I must also mention that Brian Cashman had Grandy's eyes checked by an ophthalmologist, who discovered that his eyesight wasn't quite up to par and adjusted his contact lenses. Was it the new ideas that I worked on with Grandy that caused his BA against lefties to jump to .234 in 2010? Or was it Brian's idea to get his eyes tested that made the difference? Probably depends on who you ask.

Grandy had a very strange first year in pinstripes, but what I would call a very successful one. He started slowly, and early on he lost close to a month to a pulled hamstring. And when Grandy came back, he didn't really get physically right until mid-August. Clearly, we had some work to do to get him on track. So down in Texas on an August road trip, Joe Girardi gave Grandy two full days off so that he could work with me in the cage on the things we'd started back in February, plus maybe add a few new refinements.

The bottom line, both of us agreed, was that Grandy needed to eliminate movement and shorten his swing. What we did first was get him closer to square in his stance and put his hands closer to his back shoulder in his setup. Next we evened his load by having him make a very minimal move backward with his legs and then shorten slightly his forward stride to help keep his weight centered. The last thing we tried was to have him hold on to the bat through his swing with both hands.

Midseason adjustments can be tricky, and sometimes counterproductive, but Grandy is a terrific listener with a quick grasp of what I was trying to get across. Way too much, and I mean *way* too much, fuss was made by the media of what we did together those two days. Later, Grandy explained to people in the press that what we'd done was basically what we'd been doing all year, with a few little things added, and I couldn't agree more. But after about a thousand swings in the cage, I think Grandy and I were both pretty happy with how things worked out over the next three months.

Tell me what you think. Through August 9, Curtis hit .239 with 10 homers, 33 runs batted in, 29 walks, and a .306 on-base percentage in 301 at bats. From August 12 through the playoffs, he hit .275 with 15 homers, 40 runs batted in, 32 walks, and a .378 on-base percentage in 193 at bats.

I believe the best indicator of what the Yankees and Yankees fans can expect from Curtis Granderson in the 2011 season can be found in the second set of numbers.

You can be the smartest, most knowledgeable, most technically advanced coach in the game, but if you can't convince your ballplayers to work hard on what you're teaching them, then you might as well be talking to yourself. To do that, you have to know your guys and what makes them tick. You have thirteen guys with thirteen different personalities, and with each one, you have to know which button to push to get him to do the hard work that will make him a better hitter.

A while back, I saw a sign on a bulletin board containing a single sentence that summed up perfectly my philosophy, my approach to my job. And so, when I got home, I googled it and was pleased to discover that the words came from a pretty good authority: Vince Lombardi. "The dictionary is the only place that success comes before work."

9 | WELCOME TO MY OFFICE

C ome on in. Make yourself comfortable. Pretty impressive, huh?
Bet you didn't think a major-league hitting coach's office would be anywhere near this big.

Go ahead, have a look around.

One huge room with two beautiful cages. It was built to perfection, with both cages about 80 feet by 20 feet, totaling something like 3,620 square feet. It's right behind our dugout, just down the steps, within twenty yards of the field. Talk about convenience. What an ideal spot for an office!

Shoot, Marcey and our daughter and two sons and I lived in a lot less space in the apartments we rented during the eighteen years I spent kicking around in the minors.

Not only have I never had working conditions this nice before—certainly not in the minors, of course, and not even in the old Yankee Stadium—but I have never *seen* a setup as fine as mine anywhere else in the majors. In my twenty years and counting in baseball, nothing compares to my current office. Since most of my working hours—ooops! I almost typed "waking" hours, and that wouldn't have been all that far off—are spent there, my new office digs make my workday a whole lot more pleasant and a whole lot more efficient.

By now, I'm guessing you'll have figured out that the office I've been going on about is my batting cage under Yankee Stadium, a short hike down a hallway from the clubhouse.

What's that? You want to know about the contraption that gets wheeled out to home plate before every game for BP? We call it a "turtle cage." Some teams call it a "shell cage." By whichever name, it's not the place where any serious, in-depth hitting instruction and practice takes place. The purpose of *pregame* batting practice is to give batters a chance to loosen up, to feed their confidence on 60-mph fastballs, and to start to get their heads ready for the game that day. Period.

During batting practice, most of our guys start by hitting line drives to the opposite field, then go to pulling balls in the later rounds. I stand behind the cage all through BP. In the later rounds, I'll call out the number of outs, the count, and the number of men on base to get hitters ready for game situations. An example would be telling Jeter that there's a guy on second base and nobody out. He then tells me that that situation's too easy and promptly lines a ball into right field. You don't have to be a baseball genius to know that the batter's goal with a runner on second and nobody out is to hit a ball to the right side of the field. Even if you ground out, you advance the runner to third base, which allows the next batter to drive him in with just about anything but a K or an infield pop-up.

We have fun during batting practice. We'll yell at our batting practice pitcher to throw strikes, especially when Tony Peña is on the mound. If Panchito throws a ball or two on a rare occasion, our guys will wear him out. Derek's the best at ragging on Tony. He'll yell out that the garbage Panchito's throwing is insulting and embarrassing, and after the round D.J. will toss his bat toward the L-screen that Tony's throwing behind. That sets it off. Other guys follow suit, and before you know it bats are in the air after every round. Fortunately, all our guys have good bat control, and Tony's never been hit once.

Fact is Panchito's the best batting practice pitcher in the majors, bar none. Proof? The man holds *two* Home Run Derby titles as the pitcher at the All-Star Game. Tony was on the mound in 2004 when Miguel Tejada (then with the Orioles) edged out Lance Berkman (Astros). Last year (2010) Tony was the pitcher of record when, after going into the final round of the Derby tied, David "Big Papi" Ortiz (Red Sox) blew away Hanley Ramirez (Marlins), 11 dingers to 5. Tony also threw to Nick Swisher, but killed him by throwing him balls down and away. Swish and all the other Yankees coaches wore Tony out, especially when Ortiz won. Nice goin', Panchito! Way to get Big Papi locked in! How come you set *him* up to win? (We all love Tony and he knows it.)

We'll also have contests and competitions going on most of the time. It might be the number of total bases a guy generates in four swings—a double, single, HR, and single would be eight total bases. We might do total RBIs with two outs, a 3–2 count, and the bases loaded. Anything to break up the everyday monotony and have some fun. The guys love it.

Because I'm left-handed, I'll usually pitch BP if we're facing a lefty that day. I enjoy it, but I do have to control my competitive instincts. BP is about guys getting ready for the game, not about my trying to run my cutter past them. But now and then, I'll lose a little control and throw a couple of tough pitches that my hitters don't like. Swisher usually yells at me to fix my chip. I have several bone chips floating around in my elbow that on occasion affect my control. What I really want to do is groove it down the middle, so players can swing the bat well.

But my serious teaching doesn't take place from behind the BP cage. It takes place back in my office.

Take a closer look.

Brand-new nets . . . long and wide cages . . . beautiful turf . . .

L-screens (I'll explain them in a minute) . . . tees . . . a shiny new Iron Mike machine . . . a curveball machine (more on that later, too) . . . and big baskets of pearly white baseballs bearing the official seal of the American League and the signature of Allan H. "Bud" Selig, commissioner of baseball.

Spacious bathrooms? Windows with views of the South Bronx? Pictures of the Babe, the Iron Horse, Joltin' Joe, Scooter, Yogi, Mick, and other Yankees heroes lining the walls? Comfy chairs? Sorry, none of the above, but who cares? We don't need any of that. We just need time and focus to make things happen. This is where we get after it; this is where we fine-tune swings; this is where we use drills to build muscle memory. The more times he repeats his swings properly in the cage, the more apt a player is to carry them onto the field without even thinking about them when he steps up to the plate and forty-five thousand fans are yelling their heads off.

You can't teach hitting from the dugout. You can't teach hitting during a game. You can only *teach* hitting in the cage. My office. (No regular office hours, by the way. My office door's always open. You wanna work on something? Let's go.)

Honestly, the time I spend in my office with my players is more valuable than anything else I do. During a game, of course, I watch every swing of every at bat by every Yankee. But if I see something wrong, I can't very well call "Time out!" and run up to the plate to adjust a guy's stance by a couple of inches. (At least I've never tried that tactic. Yet.)

By the way, when we're in the field and the other guys are taking their cuts, you won't spot me on the bench relaxing and watching the game. Matter of fact, I have *never* seen an entire home game in my four years with the Yankees, and I know I never will see one. That'll have to wait until I retire.

Not that I'm not interested, mind you, but when we're out in the field, I'm back in our video room dissecting what just took place in our half of the inning. That way, if Brett Gardner or somebody comes back in and starts asking me what happened on that fourth pitch, the one he dribbled out to second, I'm in a position to give him some informed feedback that might help him the next time he's up. Almost every one of our guys will ask me something during the game. Sometimes it might be pitch selection, other times it might be about a component of his actual swing. Because of my work in the video room, I'll usually have a concrete answer based on something I've seen.

A major-league hitter knows how easy it is to slide into bad habits, like extending his hands to reach for the ball. On the bench during a game, I keep a chart of every at bat for every player, and you better believe that I try to be as precise as possible. I track a lot of information that helps me determine when a guy is truly struggling or just needs a bit of luck. A lot of times, a guy can be swinging the bat well and have nothing to show for it. My job is to assure him that he's taking good cuts and that things will go his way if he just keeps on keeping on.

When a player's swing deserts him temporarily and he starts to struggle, I'll approach him and suggest that maybe he ought to come by my office to work on a few things. Or maybe he'll come to me: "C'mon, K-Long, I've got to figure out what the &$%#!@ I'm doing. I feel like a @!#%$& &$%#!@ up there."

However we get there, once we're in my office I do a lot of watching and listening before I do any talking. A lot of the time, the player will figure it out himself and just look over to me for confirmation. Sometimes we get it over with in five minutes. It'll be like, "Yeah! Of course! I was opening up too much. I got it!" And just like that, he's ready to go back out and hit line drives. Other times, it can take hours, even days to identify the problem and solve it. If a guy's willing to work, he *knows* I'll be with him every step of the way. This is what we call grinding until the swing comes back. Everyone in baseball goes through it, some just more than others.

My best example is with Jason Giambi in 2008. He was swinging the bat well, his mental approach was good, and he was swinging at strikes, but he couldn't find a hole. In other words, his luck was just flat out bad. His quality at bats, hard-hit balls, and every other thing I use to measure success were at good levels. At this point the media, the fans, and even ownership were wondering if Jason was done. I kept telling everyone that according to my data the Big G was doing things right, and that his luck would turn around. As bad of a start as Jason had, his year ended up pretty good: 36 HRs and 92 RBIs, with a .247 BA. As of 2010 Jason was still playing but in a limited role with the Colorado Rockies.

Every hitter in the game goes to the plate with the numbers stacked heavily against him. In 2009, the overall batting average was .259 in the National League, .267 in the American League because of the DH. That means the pitcher's going to win almost 70 percent of the time. Not good odds for the guy with the piece of wood in his hands, and he can't afford to do anything, *anything,* to make them worse.

Let me put it another way. In a 162-game season, a starting player's going to see more than three thousand pitches. And sure, he's going to have some tough days, even tough weeks. But the more he can maximize solid basics, the more of those pitches he's going to turn into something good. I believe that quality time spent with me in the cage will help him get there.

What all goes on in my office?

That varies from player to player, from problem to problem, so we have different drills to help with different parts of the swing. Each player has his own routine, his own set of things he likes to work on. And, of course, I'm likely to throw in a suggestion or two now and then.

Let's go through the range of options.

THE TEE

I'm big on hitting off the tee. I don't know this for a fact, but my guess is that the Yankees use the tee more than any other team in the majors.

Most of the players on our team use the tee regularly, some of them religiously. All of them like to start with the tee just to get loose before they move to the toss drill. For a few guys, once they're loose, they move on. But most spend a lot of time with the tee because it can be used in so many ways.

Set up high to help guys keep their hands up and work on top of the ball. (One of the most harmful and most common swing flaws in my book is to drop your hands before the pitch.)

Set up low to help them work down and through the ball.

Inside corner, outside corner, and so on.

If I'm working with someone on the tee, I'll set it up smack in the middle of home plate, which is where you want contact between bat and ball to occur. Kneeling at the side facing the hitter, I place a ball on the tee, and the hitter repeats his swing over and over and over again at precisely the perfect contact point. The tee's great because we can create high pitches, low pitches, outside pitches, inside pitches, and right down the middle pitches simply by adjusting the height and position of the tee.

The tee gives me an up-close-and-personal look at the hitter's feet, legs, midbody, and hands. If anything's out of kilter, it's easy to spot. Exactly how I transmit a flaw to a guy is sometimes not as easy as spotting it, but by repeating contact points over and over we usually get it right.

You can learn more about your swing hitting off a tee than from hitting live pitching, and a *lot* more than from hitting off a pitching machine. The idea is that you build good habits hitting off the tee. These habits, having to do with your stance and your hand positioning and so on, become second nature, so that you take them up to the plate with you, without even thinking about it. When a guy's bringing 95-mph heat, you don't want to be thinking about whether your feet are lined up right. You want to be thinking about one thing and one thing only: seeing the ball.

(By the way, with the wildfire-like growth of T-ball in Y-run programs across the country, kids as young as three or four can begin to groove good swings before they encounter their first lobs in Pee Wee ball.)

Ten or eleven of my thirteen position players hit off the tee before every game. *Every* game. And I'm right there, watching every swing. A perfect session? When I don't say a single word, or make a single suggestion, because there's no need to.

FRONT TOSS

This is the most popular drill in baseball cages throughout the majors. It's the one that I bet every player in the big leagues uses daily. I know it's the drill that I employ most often, in no small measure because that's what my players want.

This drill is performed with what's called an "L-screen" set about seven or eight yards from home plate. What I do is show the hitter the ball, then step and toss it to him underhand, then step back behind the long part of the "L" so I don't get killed. By the way, I probably shouldn't use the word *toss,* because anybody who has ever taken a flip off me knows that I don't toss it, *I fire it!*

Because I believe that hitters need to get ready and into the hitting position early, I force them into doing that by flipping, ah, rather *firmly.* Don't take this the wrong way. I'm not trying to strike guys out. (Fat chance!) I just want them to stay centered and not push or go get the ball. I want them to be ready and in a good position to react to the ball.

From my vantage point in front of and close to the batter, I can check out his body alignment (*Square!*) and the position of his hands (*Back!*) before the toss. Then, as he swings through the ball, I watch to see how his body and hands react throughout contact. I watch his body for any swaying, his head for any extra movement, and his eyes to make sure they're following the ball.

After ten to fifteen pitches, we'll stop and I'll tell him what I've seen. Typically, I'll ask him to concentrate on only one thing for the next set, and then we'll do ten to fifteen more pitches. Another conference, and maybe another ten to fifteen, depending on whether somebody else might be hanging around waiting his turn.

Another thing: I truly believe that the guy waiting to hit next in the cage can learn a great deal by just watching and listening. Every suggestion I offer up is a positive one—always "Do this," never "Don't do that"—and since the basics of hitting are, in my view, the same for everyone, hearing them repeated will sink into the subconscious of everyone in earshot.

The days of throwing batting practice in the cages are fading fast. Not fast enough in my book. You'll save your coach's arm with front toss, plus once you get the hang of flipping properly, it becomes very easy to throw strikes and spot the ball. You can do this on the field as well; we do a lot of it outside in spring training.

(You Little League and high school coaches reading this, just remember to flip firmly; don't lob it in there with a hump. Your players aren't going to see anything like that in a game.)

NET DRILL

This is a modified version of front toss in which the hitter stands one bat length away from the net enclosing the cage. I move the screen over so I'm dead in front of him about seven or eight yards away, and I offer up a firm underhand toss between him and the net. This drill emphasizes staying tight to your core and staying inside the ball. With the net so close to his body, I've found that the hitter stays square, stays back better, and uses his lower half and hands properly. It's a pull drill that a lot of my players call the "homer drill." Most home runs are hit to the pull-side gap, and this drill gets guys in position to hammer balls to the pull side without letting their swing get too long. In all my years of using this drill, I've had only a few guys pull balls foul. It's virtually impossible because of the net's proximity to the hitter. A long drive into the upper deck that goes foul may produce a few oohs and aahs, but it doesn't change the score.

SHORT BAT

The short bat is just that—a twenty-nine- or thirty-inch bat that we use to shorten the distance to contact. Most of our guys will use the short bat from time to time during their drill work. Most guys use just one hand. They'll work their bottom hand first, then top hand, and usually finish with both hands. A few guys just use two hands the whole time.

Some players use the short bat off the tee; others prefer to have me flip to them. Either one is fine, but if you're teaching your son or daughter how to hit, just make sure the tee or flips are in tight to the body. The worst thing you can do is to get the ball out away from the body; it defeats the purpose of teaching a player to keep his arms close in so that he doesn't overextend his arms.

SIDE TOSS

In this drill, I stand to the side of the hitter and toss the ball directly at him. I don't use this one very often, but it can be beneficial in helping a player find a deep contact point. By flipping the ball from the side, I can toss the ball at the hitter's belly button and keep him back and short to the ball. If I'm tossing from the side, he's forced to wait to swing until the ball crosses deep into the hitting zone and not get out in front.

PITCHING MACHINE

You may be a little surprised to learn that we employ the pitching machine only about 10 percent of the time, maybe less. Our guys like the other drills a lot more; so do I. The machine has some utility for working on hitting the curveball, but that's about it. In fact, we have the machine set up for curveballs only.

A little strange, if you think about it, because a top-quality pitching machine costs about two thousand dollars, whereas a hitting tee costs sixty bucks.

* * *

When it comes to cage work, one size does *not* fit all.

Robinson Cano and Nick Swisher love to do the net drill on the field, and they'd probably do it every day if I let them. They usually take tons of swings, which gives them the feeling they're looking for, and that'll hold them over for about a week. But I don't let them do it every day or they'd simply be too exhausted to play.

Jorge Posada, a switch-hitter, is a tee-only guy left-handed and a front toss guy right-handed before games.

Derek Jeter does tee first, then no-stride front toss, during which he incorporates his regular tap and leg kick toward the end. He also loves to take BP on the field; on days when we have to cancel it, typically because of wet field conditions, he can get monumentally irritated with me. What can you say? The guy just flat out *loves* to hit.

Mark Teixeira starts a typical fifteen-minute session in my office hitting off the tee (five to six minutes), then goes to front toss (four to five minutes), and finishes with the net drill (three to four minutes). As the season wears on, Tex will drop down to two, sometimes to just one of the three drills, depending on how he's going and what he thinks he needs to work on.

Tex uses the tee the same way every day. He starts with it very high and smack in the middle of the plate. The idea: work on keeping his hands up and on top of the ball. Then he lowers the tee to thigh high. The idea: work different zones, starting with inside and finishing with away. Next and last, he positions the tee low, at the very bottom of the hitting zone. The idea: work on staying down and through the ball.

After his work with the tee and front toss, Tex usually finishes with about fifteen swings from each side of the plate with the net drill.

Tex might vary his drill slightly from day to day, but he generally sticks to this basic program. Hey, it works for him. The last two seasons (2009–10), he averaged 36 homers and 115 ribbies.

* * *

Left to right: Britney, Kevin, Marcey, Tracy, and Jaron (*front*) in Memphis, Tennessee, August 1993.

Left to right: Marcey, Tracy, Jaron, Kevin, and Britney, Christmas 2002. *(Thompson Photographic)*

Left to right: Tracy, Jaron, Marcey, Kevin, Britney, Jackson, and Mark, November 2010. *(Images for a Lifetime)*

Marcey and Kevin, just after the Wildcats beat the Sundevils during Kevin's senior year at the University of Arizona, 1989.

Marcey and Kevin on their wedding day, 1990.

Kevin and Marcey at home in Arizona during the off-season, 2004.

(*Thompson Photographic*)

Kevin in his Pop Warner Blackhawks football uniform with his dad, Gary Long, 1978.

Kevin in his Thunderbird High School football uniform during his senior year, 1985.

Kevin and Marcey's dad, Dennis Peed, shortly before he passed away in 2006.

From top to bottom: Kevin chatting with Robinson Cano during batting practice, 2008; Kevin and Andy Pettitte celebrating after the Yankees' 2009 World Series win; batting practice at Yankee Stadium, 2009. (*Yankees/Ariel Goldman*)

Celebrating an A-Rod walk-off home run in 2009.
Left to right: Hideki Matsui, Phil Coke, Kevin Long, Alex Rodriguez, and Robinson Cano.

Kevin with his college buddies and teammates. *Left to right:* J. T. Snow, Trevor Hoffman, Lance Dickson, Kevin Long, and Scott Erickson.

Kevin with Harvey Kuenn, manager of the Milwaukee Brewers, during Kevin's time as a spring training batboy, 1982.

Kevin working with the grounds crew during his second year with the Wilmington Blue Rocks, 1998

Kevin and Jaron at the Wilmington Blue Rocks field, 1997.

Kevin with Coach Kindall at a University of Arizona alumni game, 2003.

Kevin hanging out with first-base coach Mick Kelleher (*left*) and third-base coach Rob Thomson (*center*) at the All-Star Game, 2010.

Kevin's mother, Donna Van de Water; Marcey; Kevin; and Grandma Jane before his first Opening Day ever at the old Yankee Stadium, 2007.

Kevin with his grandson, Jackson, on the field before a game, 2010.

Joba Chamberlain, Andy Pettitte, Alex Rodriguez, and Kevin with Tommy Ellenson during Hope Week 2009.

(Yankees/Ariele Goldman)

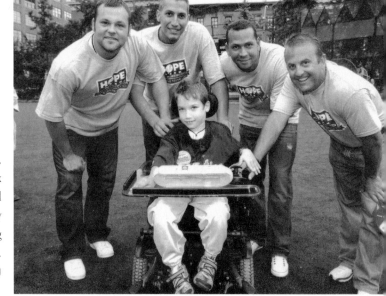

For night games at home, which generally have a 7:05 P.M. start, I'm in the Yankees clubhouse, all suited up and ready to go, no later than 1:00 P.M. For day games, with the first pitch at 1:05 P.M., I'm there at around 8:00 A.M. Sometimes, if a player has asked for a little extra time—or if I think he needs it and he's agreeable—I might get in earlier. Very occasionally—make that very, very *rarely*—a player looking for some help will get to the clubhouse before I do. I hate that. As I told you in the preceding chapter, I like to think of myself as one of the hardest workers in the house. When somebody's waiting to see me when I arrive for work, I want to kick my own butt. Fortunately, that doesn't happen often, and when it does, it's almost always because I'm in some meeting that we coaches are required to attend. My motto, my mantra, my guiding principle: *Always Be There When a Guy Wants to Work.*

Sure, I'm prejudiced, but I consider my Yankees hitters to be the hardest workers in the game. They get in their cage work almost every day. They stagger themselves perfectly throughout the two hours leading up to BP on the field, always respecting the time limits so that the next guy gets his fair share of cage time. And, hot or not, my guys make sure to follow the daily cage routine that we've worked out.

A big part of my job is to tailor a player's routine according to his needs, his personality, his strengths, *and* his weaknesses. The operating idea—this won't come as a big surprise—is that the more precise and consistent you are with your routine and work, then the better you'll be in the game.

When a player's riding a hot streak, I make sure he gets his routine work done in the cage, then I stay out of his way unless he asks a question. Guys in slumps, you won't be surprised to learn, come by to try to figure out what they can do to get back in a good groove. On a rare occasion a guy will skip a day to charge his batteries and give his body and mind a break. I generally leave him alone as long as he's going good. But if a guy's going bad, and it's hurting the team, and I've spotted something I think might help, it's my job to sit him down and come up with a game plan. With our guys this doesn't happen a lot, but throughout the year there's always one or two guys struggling.

Before he can fix what's broken, a hitter in a slump must first make the right diagnosis of what he's doing wrong. Sounds pretty basic, right? Well, it should be, but it's a whole lot easier said than done. After all, a guy can't see himself doing that one little thing wrong that's suddenly turned hard line drives to left-center and right-center into hard one-hoppers to short and second. He can watch video until the cows come home and maybe still not see the tiny flaw that's causing him to miss pitches that just two weeks earlier he was crushing.

My job is to help him make the proper diagnosis, to be a second set of eyes, especially for the veteran player who already *knows* right from wrong, but who has let a little something sneak into his setup or swing without being conscious of it. Some guys want to powwow in the dugout. Others don't want me to come within ten feet of them until after a game. Either way, I have to be prepared to deliver my diagnosis and treatment recommendation in precise, clear terms.

(Quick Tip: Move up in the box a smidgeon and those one-hoppers become liners again.)

First off, I never use the word *slump*. Never. I never go up to a guy who's 5 for his last 40 and say, "Hey, dude, you're stinking the place up, so how about we spend a little extra time in the cage seeing what we can do to get you out of that miserable slump you're in."

Definitely not the recommended approach, especially since—to a man—my guys are bigger, younger, and tougher than me.

For one thing, 7 of those 40 at bats may have produced hard grounders or drives right at somebody. Had they gone through, he'd be hitting .300, not .125. Maybe the guy caught a couple of bad calls on two-strike counts. What I'm saying is that maybe he's swinging the bat well, doing all the things he's supposed to be doing right, but still only has 5 for his last 40 because . . . that's baseball.

Stats tell you a lot, but they don't tell you the whole story. Unfortunately, a lot of times the media focus *only* on the numbers. The best reporters know better; they know to look behind the numbers and see how a guy's swinging the bat. But too many times you read or hear, "Joe DiMaggio's mired in a deep slump, and the Yankees faithful are wondering if this is the beginning of the end for Joltin' Joe."

Bullshit.

Pardon me, but a whole lot of what you read and hear about so-and-so's "slump" is just that: bullshit. Or, more politely: one-dimensional and simplistic.

But the main reason for not using the S word is what it might do to the state of mind a player takes with him to the plate. If he goes up there believing he's in a slump, thinking about being in a slump, then he's starting off with two strikes against him, if you'll pardon the use of the oldest cliché the game of baseball has ever produced.

Positive.

Positive.

Positive.

That's gotta be the attitude a player *must* take with him *every* time he steps up to the plate. Alex Rodriguez has the best description of the attitude a player should take to the batter's box when he hasn't been hitting well: "Doesn't matter what I did my last time up or my last ten or my last thirty. Every time I go to the plate, I figure I'm one good swing away from batting 1.000."

That's why I never use the S word out loud. Not to a reporter who asks me what I'm going to do to get Babe So-and-So out of one. And certainly not to a player who's in an S.

Look, all hitters, even the best ones, struggle now and then. Every guy who makes his living with a bat goes through patches when he just doesn't feel good at the plate. Maybe he falls back into an old (bad) habit without realizing it. Maybe he tries to fix things with a minor adjustment only to make them worse.

My prescription? Take advantage of that second set of eyes that have studied him when he's going good and going bad. Get a second opinion.

Mine. And how do I help this guy get going again, help get him back on track, help lift him out of his S?

My method of helping a player find his swing will vary quite a bit from player to player. If a guy who's not a cage rat and doesn't like to spend a lot of time on his drills isn't going so good, I'll try showing him video or talking to him about what I'm seeing. Other times I may show him a chart of the pitches he's swinging at. A simple fly-by statement like "your hands aren't loading" or "get into your legs" sometimes triggers a thought in his mind. Or maybe I'll just say nothing, wait for him to approach me. Sometimes these indirect methods work, but to be truthful, I think his best bet is to come spend a little time with me in my office.

Anyway, that's my story and I'm sticking to it.

Our clubhouse in the new Yankee Stadium is like this giant, incredible spa. We have everything: a weight and cardio room, a steam room, a massage therapy room, a dining room, a kitchen with our own chef, six giant TV screens suspended from the ceiling, a video and games room, even a "Theatre Room." In a previous life, the theater room was just a big storage space next to the coaches' dressing room until C. C. Sabathia and Jorge Posada turned it into a mini movie theater, complete with a big-ass projection-screen TV, leather couches, and recliners. (I call it the Dark Cold Cave.) It also has plenty of blankets that see a lot of use by guys sleeping over when there's been a rain delay and a night game doesn't end until 2:00 in the morning, and we have a 1:05 start the next day.

Most ballplayers do the everyday clubhouse things exactly the same way, day in and day out. They align their gloves and gamers and shoes and other gear in their lockers just so. Most put on their unis the same way, exactly the same way, every day: sanitary socks (both feet in at the same time), then left sock, right sock, left stirrup, right stirrup, left shoe, right shoe, and so on. Not all of the guys are that rigid, of course, but a lot are, and mostly they are respected, and left alone.

Modern technology has transformed the clubhouse music scene since I got into baseball. There's still clubhouse-wide music going on all the time, really loud music courtesy of Swish, who took over from Johnny Damon as designated DJ after Johnny moved on to the Tigers. But what with everybody having iPods these days, the clubhouse music isn't as important as it used to be. In the "good old days," I've been told, guys would sometimes get in fights over what was pouring out over the loudspeakers or out of their boom boxes. Plus talking and texting on iPhones and BlackBerries has replaced a lot of the banter, back-and-forth, and bullshit that used to keep the place bubbling.

We coaches have our own drills as well. After a win, when Mike Harkey becomes DJ in the coaches' dressing room, we can count on bumping to MC Hammer's "Can't Touch This." And you can make book on Rob Thomson and Mick Kelleher heading to the steam room following our home wins for a nice long steam. (Never after a home loss, never on the road.)

One big change in the clubhouse since Joe Girardi took over in 2008 is sons being allowed to join their fathers in the clubhouse. Every home game when Jaron is in town, he tags along to Yankee Stadium with me. In the past couple of years he's pulled shifts as batboy and ball boy, and he's put in a lot of time in the video room studying swings. Plus he's spent a lot of quality time with Andy Pettitte's sons, Josh and Jared. What a terrific experience for them, thanks to Joe.

The game after an off day, we have optional early on-field batting practice. Most of the guys like to take part. These are very laid-back sessions where guys can get in some extra swings and have some fun doing it. Derek and Jorge never miss early BP. Joba Chamberlain, A. J. Burnett, and Andy Pettitte like to come to these early BP sessions to shag balls and goof around in the outfield.

A lot of the stuff that goes on before the first pitch or in the clubhouse after a win is a reminder of what baseball really and truly is—a game. That's why I love my job so much.

At the end of the day, after all, it's not modern technology and spaciousness and creature comforts that matter. The two things that make for a great clubhouse are the personalities of twenty-five guys and the size of the number in the W column at the end of the season. Based on those two criteria, what we have up in the Bronx is a *great* clubhouse.

The best in baseball.

My job starts with direct, effective communication. Some players may need a nudge to work a little harder; others may need me to back off. Even the best players in the world struggle at times, but if I pay attention to each individual and his needs, it becomes a fixable problem. I can't say it enough: "Put the time in and you can fix it." And if a guy wants to come in at 6:00 in the morning the next day, or get it right after a game, I'll cancel all my plans and be there. Am I open for business 24/7? No, not quite, but it sometimes feels like it.

We closed the cages only once in my four years with the Yankees. That was in Toronto in 2007, when Joe Torre said, "No hitting today." Sometimes things are going so bad, and you search for anything to get your team back on the winning ways. In this case Joe believed a day away from the cages was just what we needed. I don't remember how we did that day, but I can tell you it was the hardest thing I've ever had to do.

I have thirty (there are thirty major-league teams) branch offices all around the country. Not one is as fine as the one in Yankee Stadium, of course. A few of the ballparks—Toronto, Cleveland, Tampa, L.A. (the Dodgers), and Chicago (White Sox)—have only one indoor cage, which is a real pain in the butt, because we have to share and can get in only one hour of work before BP. I just have to make that hour as focused as it can possibly be.

Guys occasionally want to come in to do some work on their off days. (My off days, too, if you're scoring at home.) My answer is always the same: no problem; meet you there.

Always a sluggish starter, Tex got off to an especially slow start in

2010 and asked me if he could get in some extra BP on an off day in late April. We were in Tampa, so it was easy to go over to our minor-league complex. Off day or no off day, I really enjoyed it. Tex is the consummate professional and someone I respect and enjoy hanging out with, so why not spend some quality time together? What else was I going to do? Play golf? Look, I'm a baseball junkie who loves his job, so give me a baseball field over a golf course any day.

In 2009, the day after we'd completed a sweep of the Twins 3–0 in the AL Division Series, Johnny Damon called me on my cell and said he'd like to come in and "work on a few things." Seemed like a good idea to me: Johnny had gone 1-for-12 in the three games (.083), and it hadn't been a pretty 1-for-12. Our middle-innings reliever Alfredo Aceves and spot starter Chad Gaudin needed some work and were going to throw a simulated game at the stadium. We had our extra position players coming to the stadium to hit and Johnny was going to join them. He took three or four at bats that day, spent three minutes, tops, ripped a few line drives, and hit a home run off Alfredo. Then, in typical J.D. style, he said, "Okay, guys. Thanks. That should do me."

Turns out he was right: in the ALCS (against the Angels) and the World Series (Phillies), Johnny hit a combined .327 with 2 homers and 9 RBIs. I guess you could call that off day well spent.

(Now if I could just figure out some way to take a little bit of credit for J.D.'s three stolen bases against the Phils . . .)

Young guys who are new to the majors, guys like Ramiro Peña and Francisco Cervelli, need my help most. My biggest challenge is to help them remain at the big-league level—no easy task, since the majority of major leaguers get sent back to the minors within their first full year.

Cervi got his first call to the big leagues in September 2008 when rosters expanded, but he was back in AA Trenton in 2009. Then he got another shot when Jorge Posada went on the DL. Cervi's job would be to catch twice a week to give our regular backup catcher, José Molina, a rest. My job was to help turn a kid hitting .190 in AA into a consistent major-league hitter.

The good news was that Cervi wouldn't be playing every day, which meant we had a lot of time to spend in the cage. After a couple of sessions, we concluded that Cervi needed to shorten his swing, create more bat speed by using his lower half, overhaul his mechanics, and create a solid daily routine that he could understand and feel good about.

And so we went to work.

Every day we did the same thing. He always got to the cage early, and he always came ready to put in the time and effort needed to become more consistent. We got him to spread out, get more flexion in his lower half, keep his torso upright, employ a minimal stride, and work on getting his back side completely through in his swing. After just a week, Cervi was starting to limit his preswing movements, staying more centered and balanced, and creating bat speed by using his lower half properly. Most important, he was clearly feeling good about his swing.

See why I love my job?

Cervi ended up hitting .298 in 94 at bats in 2009. In 2010, in an expanded role as Posada's regular backup, Cervi hit .271 in 266 at bats and drove in 38 runs. Not too shabby for a young catcher rushed to the majors for his defensive skills.

Great job, Cervi! But remember . . . you're not done!

10 | ADDITION BY SUBTRACTION

My philosophy with the Yankees hitters I work with is to add by subtracting. That's so important I'm going to say it again: *add by subtracting.*

Look, at the major-league level, I'm working with guys who have basically figured it out. I look for the little things. If these guys had big things wrong with their swings, they wouldn't be in the major leagues. Can they get better? Sure, some of them can, especially the younger ones, or there wouldn't be any need for people like me. But my main job is helping them fix the little things in their swings that get broken. I don't see myself as adding on new, top-secret techniques or teaching them new, revolutionary tricks. As I said, I look for the little things.

I'm patient. I don't panic. I'm consistent. I listen. I'm open. I'm always around, day or night, to work with a guy. And I try to get to know the guys I'm working with, know them personally. If I don't know who they are, have a feel for what makes them tick, how am I going to help them?

By the way, when I talk in this chapter about "*my* hitting philosophy" and what "*I* do," you're going to find that most of the time it's "we," not "I." There's a simple reason for that, and it's not because I'm a shrinking violet, or because I'm trying to con somebody by pretending to bring them into the thinking process when in fact I have some master plan that I'm trying to impose on them. And it's certainly not because I'm using the "royal we."

Look, I use "we" most of the time when I talk about working with a hitter because it reflects reality: the player and I are trying to work *together* to figure out a solution, a fix, to some problem. It's a "we" deal, not an "I" deal. If the player's not fully engaged, if he's not part of the "we" in this effort, then there's not a damned thing "I" can do to fix what's broken.

Sometimes—say, with guys like Alex and Derek and Tex—it's mostly keeping a close eye on them every single at bat so I can remind them if they get away from something they know they should be doing. With Alex, we're always monitoring the height of his leg kick and making sure he stays tight to contact. With Derek, we're always checking his stride direction and making sure he uses his legs. With Tex, we're always making sure he gets into the hitting position on time and stays tight to his core with his swing.

Something else may pop up now and again that requires our attention, but usually with these three guys we're just monitoring and fine-tuning. Think about it: if they had a bunch of things wrong with their swings, they wouldn't be the All-Stars they are. Not to say that there might not be other things going on, but usually the same symptoms will show up with these guys—and we're pretty quick to ID and fix them.

But it's also a blast to work with guys who have an abundance of talent along with a commitment to achieve greatness but haven't quite put it all together. Nothing is more satisfying as a coach than to work hard on a player's hitting techniques and his psychological approach to the game and have it pay big dividends.

No current Yankees fan will soon forget what Nick Swisher did in the 2009 World Series. Swish had a tough playoff run, and we needed to make an adjustment in a hurry—just two days to isolate the problem and fix it. Swish wasn't scheduled to start in Game 2 of the

World Series, but Joe was planning to have him in the starting lineup in Game 3.

My response? Nick, meet me in my office. Pronto.

What we did first was spread him out and get him squared up. That pretty much eliminated his stride, which enabled him to see and react better to off-speed stuff. Swish had been getting a steady diet of off-speed pitches and was really having a tough time. To Swish's credit, he was willing and able to make the adjustment, and he went on to play a big part in our Game 3 win with a double and a home run.

A hitting coach can't ask for anything more.

There was a lot more basic training to be done, naturally, when I worked with minor leaguers. A lot more interaction, a lot more "hands-on" teaching. I used to tell the kids I was seeing for the first time in A ball, "Look, my goal isn't to get you to AA. My goal isn't to get you to AAA. My goal is to help you acquire and master the tools that will get you to the majors and help you stay there."

Now and then, I'd have a kid who I was sure would take off. He'd have great physical tools: strength, bat speed, and a great eye. He looked like a natural standing at the plate. But he just didn't get it. I'd pound into him the importance of a solid base, a squared-up stance. He'd nod, yeah, yeah, okay, but the very next game, he'd be up there closing his stance, putting himself in a bad position to react to the baseball. The reality is a guy could go 4-for-4 and might be having some success and I'd have to say to him, "Look, you're sliding into the ball; you're pushing off your back side. You're getting your hits *now,* but we need to keep you centered and behind the baseball some more." He'd nod, but he was thinking about that 4-for-4, not what I was telling him. I might as well have been telling the wind to change directions.

That's the toughest part about coaching in the minor leagues. Sometimes a kid could be having some success but deep down you know he needs to make some changes or he'll struggle as he moves up. That's always been a strength of mine, the ability to be subtle but stern about what needed to be done. This is where being creative and positive with your teaching becomes vital.

A guy would be rolling along, getting his hits, and pushing his BA toward the good side of .300. Meanwhile his swing was long, the hits were soft, he wasn't driving the ball, and his strike zone discipline was atrocious. My job was to stay positive but somehow get across to him what he needed to do to become a better and more consistent hitter.

That's not an easy conversation to have with a guy who's been a big stud on his high school or college teams, a guy who's pretty sure he knows everything about the game of baseball, the way we all did when we were that age. He's just had a perfect day at the plate, and here's this old dude—I was twenty-nine, thirty at the time—who never even had so much as a cup of coffee in the major leagues telling him what he's doing wrong.

As I said, not an easy conversation.

Sometimes, I'd come up with another way of saying the same thing and—bingo!—the message would get through. Light goes on in dark room. Oh, so *that's* what you want me to do, K-Long. Okay, I get it now. Like this, right? Next thing you know it's, "Fasten your seat belts, people, we're ready for takeoff."

And other times? I've had teams when everyone hit to his natural ability but one guy, and it tore me up. I truly care about every guy on the team and want the best for each individual.

Well, those other times kept me awake at night.

Still do.

See the ball.

Pretty basic, right? If you can't see the ball, you can't hit it, at least not consistently, not with authority. And if you have a big stride and create forward movement, the rest of your body (including your head!) is going with it. Maybe it doesn't feel like that's happening, but it is. The result?

If your head's moving just a fraction, then you're not going to see the ball as well as you need to in order to hit it consistently, hit it with authority.

Control your body. Control your head. See the ball.

As I said, pretty basic.

And as I also said earlier, and as I'm likely to say again because it's the keystone of my coaching philosophy, I'm in the business of subtraction. Subtracting bad habits, that is, the worst of which is moving your body from the starting position to the time of explosion.

Addition by subtraction.

I do clinics for Little League and high school coaches during the off-season, and from time to time I'll hear from guys who'd been to the clinic the year before that they'd tried that one core, basic, fundamental approach I preach—addition by subtraction—and that it had worked. Nothing makes me feel better than hearing that. After all, we're all doing the same job, just in a different arena.

Q: What's the best way to hit a breaking ball?
A: By not missing the fastball.

That one's got to date back to "Take Me Out to the Ball Game," but it's just as true today as it was in 1934. (That's when Wikipedia thinks "Take Me Out . . ." was first played at a major-league ballpark.) No less an authority than George Brett has said that of his first 3,000 hits, 2,999 came on fastballs. A slight exaggeration, perhaps? Sure. But Brett's basic point is clear enough: always sit dead red. If you're looking for a fastball, you can adjust if you get something crooked. Look for a breaking pitch, though, and the ball will be in the catcher's mitt before you can activate Plan B.

Your mind-set should be that the pitcher's going to throw you a fastball right down the middle. You sit on his slider because it's his best pitch, and that opens the door for the guy to

> *get an average-speed fastball by you. You can adjust if you're*
> *sitting on a fastball and get an off-speed pitch.*
> *But vice versa? No way.*

Can I get a player I'm working with to buy into a game plan? One that I believe will help him get the most out of his talent, help make him better? That's the constant challenge. And if I've learned one thing in my fourteen years of on-the-job learning as a coach, it's that I can't come across as an arrogant smart-ass who has a one-size-fits-all program. That'll turn off any guy. Instead, I'm watching every little thing that he does, and I'm reporting back to him what I see. I want him to feel like we're seeing his swing simultaneously, together, as a single unit. I have to convince a guy I'm working with that we're working *together*. I have to get him to understand that he may be the one taking the cuts, but I'm his biggest fan.

Do I have a system? Yes.

Am I confident that it will help? Yes.

But am I his boss? No. He's the boss.

I'm working for him, not the other way around.

11 | THE HARDEST THING

Hitting a baseball—I've said it a thousand times—is the hardest thing to do in sport."

No less an expert on the subject than Ted Williams wrote those words in his 1970 masterpiece, *The Science of Hitting,* and they're as true today as they were forty years ago. His credentials? How about 521 career home runs, 1,839 RBIs, and a lifetime BA of .344? The man did know a thing or two about hitting.

Read his book. Or if you read it a long time ago, read it again. Let me tell you, that book is full of wisdom about the art—Ted Williams called it a science, and that's right, but it's also an art form—of hitting a baseball.

I know I mentioned this earlier but it's worth saying again: the average major-league ballplayer in 2010 failed to get a base hit about seventy-five times in every one hundred at bats. That's right: the combined batting average in the American League in 2010 was a puny .260. (In the National League, without the DH, it was even worse: .255.) That means a *topflight* hitter, a guy who hits .300 or more, fails seven out of ten times. Think about that. Hit .300 and you're likely to make an All-Star team or two. Maybe even make it to the Hall of Fame, if enough of those hits are home runs. You succeed while failing to reach your goal 70 percent of the time! Can you think of any other sport where you're considered a great success if you fail "only" 70 percent of the time? Neither can I.

So if *hitting* is that tough, what about *teaching* hitting?

Welcome to my world.

Let me start by saying flat out that I don't pretend to have all the answers, and I know that I never will. What I do know after twenty years of watching and studying and experimenting and asking questions and trying different things is that I am beginning to develop a fair sense of what works and what doesn't when trying to hit a baseball.

Hey, maybe with another twenty years I *will* get it all figured out. But you know what? Even if that fine day should ever come to pass, the best hitters are *still* going to fail seven times out of ten.

That's the nature of my challenge.

Everybody knows something about baseball. Sure, pro football's a bigger "industry" today. (Good name for the NFL.) Pro basketball's way bigger than it was when I was growing up. (So are the players.) Soccer's on a surge in elementary and secondary schools because all you need is a ball, a large, flat surface, and a couple of nets. (The World Cup gave it a big boost last year. If only our guys had made it into the quarter-finals . . .) But baseball is still America's National Pastime. Always has been, always will be. (I hope.)

Ask any dad you know, and there's a pretty good chance he played some Pee Wee or Little League ball, or maybe even junior high or high school ball. None of the above? Then at least he got his pants dirty in some sandlot games here and there.

The role of moms in baseball has expanded, too. When I was a Little Leaguer, moms were pretty much restricted to the stands where their only job was to cheer for Junior even if he struck out on three pitches he never should have swung at in the first place. Today, you find more and more moms yelling encouragement from the bench as assistant coaches.

And girls in Little League? Sure, why not? As of 2010, there were about 100,000 girls playing Little League Baseball across the country, with another 350,000 or so playing Little League Softball. My good friend Andy Goulder, whom I mentioned earlier in the book, has five kids, the youngest a girl named Gracie. Gracie Goulder played baseball up until she was in seventh grade and participated in just about all my Longball Camps. She was as good if not better than a lot of the boys. The experience paid off: she got a full ride to play softball at the University of Georgia. Good going, Gracie!

So now that I have the whole family's attention, let's get started on learning how to do the hardest thing to do in sport.

Baseball players are creatures of habit who rarely if ever detour from their everyday routines once they arrive at the ballpark. That's especially true for hitters when they go up to the plate. Pay close attention the next time you're out at the ballpark.

A player might take a monster swing from his heels before stepping in . . . or knock the mud off his spikes four times (left-right, left-right) even on a dry August day . . . or pull and tug on every piece of his uniform as if he had some raging itch . . . or rock his head side to side to loosen up a nonexistent monster crick in his neck . . . or fiddle with his batting gloves, closing and opening, closing and opening them until you're thinking to yourself that the Velcro's going to wear off . . . or hold his back hand up to the umpire while he digs in . . . or stare off into the distance as if looking for divine inspiration.

Whatever it is, no matter how weird or complicated (or simple and straightforward, though you don't see them so often), whatever he does getting set his first at bat, no matter how much time it takes, you can bet the house that he will do the very same thing every at bat he takes for the rest of the game.

Game, hell—for the rest of his career.

The point is that players have their own special way to approach the plate, and that approach can vary as much as their swings. Today, players even come out to their own songs over the PA in their home ballparks. I can tell you that they spend all kinds of time thinking about what song they want playing as they walk to the plate. Anything that makes them feel sexy is what they want to hear. (But, unlike the mud knocking and uni tugging and whatnot, the song may evolve along with their taste in music.)

Okay, so that's the way *they* want to get ready to hit. Fine. Do your thing, guys. Now let me tell you the mental, emotional, and psychological approach that I, Kevin Long, want to see them take to the plate.

1. **Be Prepared:** The Boy Scouts got it right 101 years ago, and it's still right today. And where does a New York Yankees hitter go to get prepared? That's right: my office. (See Chapter 9, "Welcome to My Office.")

2. **Focus:** Those fifty-five thousand screaming fans? They're not there. You and the pitcher are the only people in the universe that matter.

3. **Believe in Yourself:** All that hard work in the cage? Here's where it pays off. You're *better* than that guy sixty feet, six inches away. You *are* going to drive the ball hard. End of story.

4. **Stay C-a-a-l-m:** Game on the line? Nah, it's just BP. Relax and swing the bat the way you know how.

5. **Get a Pitch to Drive:** Be patient. You'll get one.

6. **Stay in the Middle of the Field:** That's where the hits are.

7. **Take Your "A" Swing:** Anything else and you're wasting everybody's time.

8. **Sit on the Fastball:** If that principle is good enough for the likes of George Brett and Derek Jeter, it's good enough for you.

9. **Be Aggressive:** "Hit" is just about the most *active* verb in the dictionary. That's why I want my guys to approach the plate thinking like *hitters*, not like *batters*. After all, that's why I call myself a *hitting* coach, not a *batting* coach.

Let's begin with the basics: how to *get ready* to hit at the plate. And let me say at the outset that you're not going to find any big Kevin Long revelations here, any supersecrets about the art/science of hitting that I've never revealed to anyone besides my players. I'd hazard a guess that all twenty-nine of the other hitting coaches in the majors would deliver the same little sermon as me on the preparatory steps that every hitter ought to take before he swings the bat.

It all starts with the right setup. Failure to get in the proper position to hit the baseball *before* it's thrown can destroy any chance you have of hitting it with authority *after* it leaves the pitcher's hand. So pipe down at the end of the dugout and pay *close* attention.

1. GET A GRIP

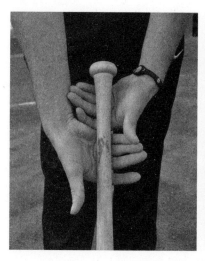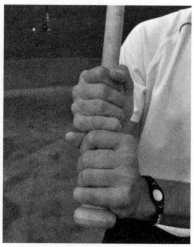

Line up the door-knocking knuckles of your hands while placing the bat in the callused part of your hands. This will help keep your grip tension-free and also reduce tension in your shoulders and elbows. By gripping the bat properly, a hitter can increase bat speed and shortness to the ball.

2. KEEP YOUR DISTANCE

Most hitters believe that setting up in the back of the batter's box gives them optimum opportunity to see the ball longer. I agree. If the hitter's rear foot is placed on the back chalk line, it gives him an extra nanosecond to track the flight of the ball. Doesn't sound like much, but against a major-league pitcher bringing 96-mph heat, every nano matters.

Think of it another way. The front edge of the pitching rubber is sixty feet, six inches from the front edge of home plate, which is seventeen inches from the back tip. Why concede those seventeen inches to the pitcher? He's got a big enough advantage as is.

3. COVER THE PLATE

Place the bat down flat on the ground perpendicular to the plate with the big end extending two inches over the outside edge. This enables you to cover the entire strike zone without reaching. It also allows you to repeat your swing without changing it by reaching or striding across your body.

4. TAKE A STANCE

Square is ideal in my book. Yes, I know there have been many great exceptions over the years, and some of them have plaques in the Hall of Fame. Stan Musial? Feet together, upper body hunched over, looked like he was peering around the corner. Joe DiMaggio? Super w-i-i-i-de stance; you'd never let a Little Leaguer set up like that.

There'll always be exceptions that prove the rule. Here are three from today's game:

- **Kevin Youkilis:** Spread your hands very far apart on the bat handle . . . start your top hand up by the label of the bat and move it up and down as the pitcher gets his sign and goes into his motion . . . hoist your hickory high above your head and point the barrel at the pitcher . . . keep your feet together and bounce up and down . . . and then, only then, as the pitcher releases the ball try to get yourself into the hitting position in time to hit a 97-mph fastball. *Guess what?* That bizarre tangle of arms, legs, and bat works great—for Kevin Youkilis. The guy with the craziest-looking stance in baseball hit .308 his last three seasons (2008–10) with the Red Sox, during which span he averaged 25 homers and 90 ribbies. (His power numbers would have been a lot higher if he hadn't missed over a third of the 2010 season because of injuries.) Sure, Kevin has the Green Monster Factor working for him, but to put up those kind of numbers with that wacko stance is a minor miracle.
- **Craig Counsell:** Hold your hands up as high as you can possibly get them . . . keep the barrel of the bat pointing straight up . . . turn your shoulders inward so that your chest is al-

most facing the umpire . . . stand as tall as you can, just short of tippy-toes. Awkward looking? That's sort of like saying the Pacific Ocean's deep. And it's only one of the weird-looking stances that Counsell's employed in his fifteen-season major-league career!

- **Ichiro Suzuki:** Pretending the bat is a sword, point it at the pitcher . . . take your top hand off the bat and rest it on your front shoulder . . . keep your feet close together and your knees even closer until the ball is on the way. Got that? Ichiro is maybe the most amazing hitter I've ever watched. He slides forward, keeps his bat on the plane longer than anyone, and seemingly is running while hitting the ball all at the same time.

But for most hitters—make that *all* the hitters I teach—square is the way to go. What exactly does square mean? It means your feet, knees, hips, and shoulders are aligned in a straight line perpendicular to the inside of the plate. The more in line you are with the pitcher, the squarer your stance is, and the easier it is to see and stay short to the ball. The shortest distance between two points is a straight line; that's why square is best.

5. BE AN ATHLETE UP THERE

"I'm not an athlete, lady," John Kruk, who forged a fine ten-year career with the Padres, Phillies, and White Sox (1986–1995), once said to a reporter. "I'm a ballplayer."

Krukie had it right, sort of, even though it might sound like he's putting himself down.

Some great ballplayers (A-Rod, Derek Jeter, Mickey Mantle, to name just three Yankees who come quickly to mind) could have made their mark in other sports. And some great ballplayers (Babe Ruth, Lou Gehrig, Yogi Berra) were . . . well, great ballplayers, period.

John Kruk (lifetime BA: .300) was a ballplayer. Nobody ever questioned that. But nobody who ever saw him walk from the dugout to home plate or rumble out to left field would also have thought, *Now there's an athlete.*

But what I try to get through to kids I work with and big leaguers alike is how much easier it is to hit from an athletic stance. I always tell kids and my players alike to give yourself the best chance to succeed.

1. Step into the box with authority.
2. Spread your feet about a bat length apart.
3. Flex your knees.
4. Bend your torso from the waist slightly if it feels right, but upright is better.
5. Stay relaxed—do *not* let your body tense up.
6. Loosen your grip slightly, then regrip—and do *not* try to extract sawdust from the barrel.

P.S.: Remember to breathe.

Look and think like an athlete up there. It'll help you be a better ballplayer.

6. IT'S NOT *ALL* IN THE HANDS . . .

. . . but a lot of it is.

I have very strong views about where the hands should be—*must* be—in a hitter's setup. (Don't believe me when I say that I have strong opinions on the subject? Just ask anybody I've ever worked with in the majors and minors.) Your hands should be about shoulder height and directly above your back knee. They should be perpendicular to your front elbow, and your front arm should be parallel to the ground and aligned with the inside edge of the plate.

Do *not* let your hands get too far away from your body.

Do *not* let them get buried too far back.

Get the picture?

7. KEEP YOUR HEAD IN THE GAME

I mean *besides* knowing the score, the count, the pitcher's strengths and weakness, how many runners are on (and how fast they are), which way the wind's blowing, the signs, all that good stuff. I'm taking for granted that you've got that covered, okay?

Tony Muser, the former manager of the Royals who currently holds the title of roving hitting instructor for the Padres, has this simple rule about where a hitter's head ought to be: "Keep your head directly over

your ass, and keep your ass positioned directly between your feet."

I would add only this: keep your head erect with both eyes looking directly at the pitcher. Remember, he's the guy trying to throw that high hard one past you. You can only hit what you can see.

8. THE RIGHT ANGLE

The right *bat angle* when setting up for the pitch, that is. My preference is forty-five degrees. Holding the bat too erect will cause a loop and upward bat path through the swing. Holding it too flat will make it harder to get to low pitches and will sometimes cause a hitter to wrap the bat around his head when he initiates the swing. Not pretty, and not effective.

incorrect bat angle

correct bat angle

But here's where I go all Mr. Softy and tell a player he has to hold the bat at an angle that feels comfortable to him and allows him the most consistent path to the baseball—as long as it's between, say, forty-three and forty-seven degrees, of course.

Ready to move on? Good. But I warn you, from this point things are going to get a little technical. Just be aware that I don't pretend to think that I can teach you how to hit here—or, if you're a Pee Wee or Little League or high school coach, how to teach somebody else how to hit. An instructional video I made with Alex Rodriguez in 2010 does a far better job of that because you get to *see* the principles of good hitting that I teach in action.

Plus you get to see my son Jaron take some mighty sweet swings illustrating the points that Alex and I are making.

Cue the Video

Over the last couple of years, a lot of people, some of whom I know pretty well, along with a bunch of baseball fans I've never met—especially Yankees fans—have called or e-mailed to tell me that I ought to write a book and make a video about hitting.

Well, now I've gone and done both.

When I first mentioned to Alex that I was thinking about filming an instructional video, his response surprised me initially, but then I realized that it was exactly what I should have expected.

Alex: "I'm in it with you . . . right?"

Me: "What? Yeah, sure. Of course. *Great!*"

Me to myself: *This guy is unreal. One of the greatest hitters of all time, someone I truly admire, and he's practi-*

cally demanding to help me put together a video? So over Super Bowl weekend in 2010, my son Jaron and I traveled to Miami and filmed a hitting video with Alex Rodriguez.

What an experience!

What an honor to have a great friend and my own son help me create this video!

What a great feeling!

And if I do say so myself, I think what we pulled off together is a pretty sweet video. But I'll let you be the judge of that:

Pro Hitter's Workout
With Kevin Long
Featuring Alex Rodriguez
Championship Productions
Available online at championshipproductions.com

Rhythm Methods

Small body and hand movements help the body relax. Fluid, under-control rhythm helps the hitter get into the proper hitting position. Just be careful not to get too many things going at one time.

1. HAND JIVE: My personal favorite: a small movement of the hands that breaks post-setup inertia and helps keep them loose. This is best explained by looking at what three Yankees do: Jeet moves his hands down, then brings them back up and cocks the bat toward the pitcher; Tex waggles his bat slowly in a circular motion; A-Rod bounces his bat slowly up and down with a slight waggle. All very different, but all very effective ways to avoid getting tense just after the setup. One thing these three different move-

ments have in common: the hands are very close to the hitting position to start with.

2. BODY SWAY: Small body sways can help a hitter avoid tension and stay relaxed. The obvious danger: rocking back and forth too much and/or too fast. Use sparingly: the more swaying and movement of the body, the harder it is to get the body in a consistent position to hit. If it were up to me, I'd take "Hand Jive" over "Body Sway" every time. But it's not up to me; it's up to my hitters. A hitting coach suggests; he doesn't dictate.

3. FINGER TALK: Some hitters waggle their fingers on the bat as a reminder not to tense up. A's center fielder Coco Crisp practically waves at the people in the boxes behind home plate.

4. TAP DANCING: A rhythmic toe tap or even a slight up-and-down movement of the heel works for some hitters.

Summary

"Different strokes for different folks." That's the operative cliché in the rhythm section, where the sole goal is to stay loose and ready to hit, whether by slight hand, body, finger, toe, or heel movements. Another tried-and-true cliché a hitter needs to keep in mind is "Everything in moderation." Too many moving parts at one time before the swing will almost certainly produce big problems later on in the swing.

Ever check out the Batting Stance Guy (Gar Ryness) on YouTube? Or his website, battingstanceguy.com? Or his new book, *Batting Stance Guy: A Love Letter to Baseball*? Do yourself a favor: turn down the corner of this page and get to know BSG right now. This guy is truly amazing at imitating baseball players' stances and swings.

In all my years, I have never, ever seen two players who were identical in how they hit, and I have never employed a cookie-cutter approach to hitting. The Batting Stance Guy confirms my wisdom regarding the uniqueness of hitting.

And he's a laugh riot, to boot.

LOAD AND STRIDE AND SEPARATE

A hitter must create a *load* . . . then *stride* . . . and then *separate* in the instant prior to swinging the bat forward. The basic idea is to get the front side ready to receive the weight of the body as the hitter swings the head of the bat toward the oncoming baseball.

LOAD

Some hitting coaches refer to this as the "Take Away." Others call it the "Trigger." Whatever the term, it means the subtle move by the hitter to get into the correct hitting position. This movement generally occurs as the pitcher separates his hands. Understand that "Load" varies ever so slightly from hitter to hitter.

Here are some different ways that different players load:

1. **Shift Weight to Back Side:** From balanced position, with weight evenly distributed on both legs, shift weight onto back leg. Create weight shift with lower half of body. Make sure not to overload—that is, don't go too far back. (A couple of role models to study: Manny Ramirez, Derek Jeter.)
2. **Leg Kick:** Picking up front leg transfers some weight to back leg. (Don't overdo it, Alex!) Leg kick must be under control and not too high. Go up and down without pushing forward or gaining distance toward pitcher. (Matt Holliday, Alex)

3. **Toe Tap:** Small tap with front foot helps hitter keep weight on back side. Tap in place or (slightly!) back. (Carlos Beltran, Jorge Posada)

4. **Tiptoe:** Picking up heel of front foot (slightly!) and going to toe (slightly!) shifts small amount of weight to back side. Effective because it eliminates any extra movement. (Albert Pujols, Brett Gardner)

5. **Front Knee Cock:** Front knee tucks inward toward back knee. Similar to "Leg Kick," but knee goes back instead of up. (Jose Reyes, Robinson Cano)

6. **Open to Square:** Start with open stance, then close to square. Allows a hitter to stay centered (or back) while preventing him from gaining distance forward with stride. (Johnny Damon, Mark Teixeira)

7. **Hand Loads:** All hitters cock their hands, some more than others. The key is to keep hands as close to hitting position as possible and allow them to load naturally. Hands that start too close to the head or too far toward the center of the body require too much movement. (Evan Longoria, Curtis Granderson)

STRIDE AND SEPARATE

These two terms taken together describe the necessary interaction of the stride foot, the body, and the hands in the split second before the hitter attacks the ball. The challenge is that so much has to go right and in sync in a very short time during "Stride and Separate," when one little tiny glitch will blow everything up. The front foot needs to be down and the body and hands must be in the proper position in order to react and put your "A" swing on the ball.

1. **Timing:** This varies slightly due to different types of loads, but most hitters stride at or slightly before release.

2. **Direction:** No variation here: the hitter must *always* stride directly at the pitcher, keeping everything square. That's best done with the front foot closed to slightly open, and the hips and shoulders closed and square. The idea is to keep the hitter on the ball as long as possible.

3. **Length:** Maintain balance during and after completion of the stride. A short controlled movement with the front foot encourages better vision, balance, and timing. The body will have some movement forward, but after the front foot goes down, the head and body should remain centered. Land with the front foot softly with the weight on balls of feet.

4. **Lower Half:** Begin stride with the legs, during which the upper body should have minimal inward coil. Maintain flexion in both legs. Weight should be evenly distributed at this point.

5. **Upper Half:** During the stride the upper body travels forward until the front foot lands. Beware of overrotating inward—it adds length to the swing and also causes visual problems. Keep torso upright; do not tilt over. Do not permit upper body to go past midpoint of body.

6. **Hands:** During "Load" and "Stride and Separate" move the hands into the proper hitting position, just off back shoulder, and get ready to fire with lower half and hands.

POSITION A+

On completion of "Load" and "Stride and Separate," a hitter should be down and ready to react to the baseball and create maximum bat speed.

1. **Weight:** Evenly distributed.
2. **Hands:** Back and off the back shoulder.
3. **Wrists:** Slightly cocked.
4. **Body:** Feet, knees, hips, and shoulders are in line.

STAY CONNECTED TO CONTACT

As the lower half begins to fire in the torque and explosion phase of the swing, the hands and back elbow stay connected and tight to the core to enable the hitter to create a short and powerful swing. The lower half of the body and the hands must rotate together.

1. **Back Foot**: Rotates and turns, but without sliding forward or away from the plate.

2. **Back Knee:** Drives down to transform back leg into an "L."

3. **Hips:** Rotate and explode in unison. The front hip clears a path; the back hip drives through it. Without hip torque and explosion, you might as well not have a bat in your hands. All great hitters have tremendous hip torque.

4. **Front Leg:** Snaps straight and firms up as hips explode. This action gives the hitter something to hit against and

keeps him on the baseball. Flexion in the front leg disappears altogether upon contact.

5. **Front Foot:** Remains closed or slightly open upon contact. Some hitters spin or open their front foot, but only after contact.

6. **Elbows:** The elbows form a triangle and remain flexed until initiation of the swing. At that point, the back elbow slides into the slot off the back hip where it remains connected to contact. The front elbow straightens out upon contact, while the back elbow maintains some flexion. *Remember: it's vital to keep elbows tight to the core and not let them work away from the body.*

7. **Hands:** In the loading or cocked position, the palms remain perpendicular to the ground with the back of the lower hand aimed at the pitcher. On initiation of the swing, the palms flatten until they're parallel with the ground at point of contact, at which point they roll: the palm of the lower hand folds until it's facing up while the palm of the upper hand folds down. *Keep the hands in tight and don't let them work out away from the body.* The

farther away from the body the hands drift, the more apt they are to roll over prematurely and come around the ball.

8. **Shoulders:** Keep them squared as long as possible. The hips and hands, if properly aligned and working in unison, will cause the front shoulder to open while the back shoulder tilts down and toward the ball.

9. **Head:** Keep head turned toward the pitcher so that the eyes can track the ball and lock on the contact point. The head should stay in place with minimal movement and not slide forward toward the ball.

10. **Down and Through:** Work *down and through* the ball during the contact phase of the swing. Working *up and off* the ball will cause a poor bat angle and add length to the swing.

down and through

working up and off the ball

The likely result: a feeble nubber back to the mound or a lazy pop-up to the infield. Or a swing and miss.

BACK SIDE AND BALANCE

Maintaining a balanced, strong back side and lower half is the single most important factor in hitting a baseball. Without a strong foundation built from the ground up, a strong, consistent swing is impossible. I always tell our guys that when the swing works in sequential order, then it is right or balanced.

1. **Back Side:** By "back side," I mean your back foot, your back knee, your hips, and your hands. They must stay tight and connected and work together in unison for a hitter to have any chance at all.

2. **Balance:** *Always* finish in a balanced position, which will occur if the swing works from the ground up and at the right effort level. In cage work and BP on the field, I tell a guy to hold his pose at the end of each swing to test whether his body's in balance. That way, in a game situation against live pitching, finishing balanced becomes second nature. And when a good hitter now and then looks awkward and unbalanced at the end of a swing? That usually means a pitcher has completely fooled him or that his mechanics are in need of a tune-up.

FINISH

The quality of the finish on a particular swing is dictated by the quality of the swing on that particular pitch. The finish is the least discussed aspect of the mechanical process of hitting a baseball for an obvious reason: the ball has already been struck (or missed).

But the finish is nonetheless a good indicator of what went right or wrong with a swing.

1. **Lower Half:** The hips have rotated so that the belt buckle is facing the pitcher. The back leg forms an "L," with the rear foot raised on the toe or ball of foot and the shoelaces facing directly toward the pitcher.

2. **Hands:** Two hands or one? High or low? These are always the focus of the biggest debates with the finish. Some good hitters release the top hand in the follow-through; others don't. Some go high at the end; others go low. There's no one-size-fits-all approach. Releasing the top hand can help a hitter stay through a pitch and stabilize his head, but the top hand must stay on the bat until the bat head gets past the front shoulder on its way toward foul territory. Keeping two hands on the bat through the swing can help a hitter stay short to contact. Some people think keeping two hands on the bat diminishes power. Not so. Both hands are always on the bat upon contact; what happens with the top hand after contact is immaterial. As to high versus low in the finish, the height of the pitch is the primary determinant of where the bat finishes, and that's in the pitcher's hands. Or was.

3. **Head and Eyes:** Stable and locked on the contact point until the finish is complete.

WHO HAS THE BEST SWING IN BASEBALL?

That's a medium fastball right down the middle. Ask just about anybody in baseball and you'll get the same answer: Twins catcher Joe Mauer. That's as near as you'll ever come to a unanimous opinion about anything. Albert Pujols and Manny Ramirez are up there, but Mauer has a picture-perfect swing. Squared up, no excess movement, never any reaching—simple, simple, simple. I remember once last summer seeing him swing and miss on an Andy Pettitte pitch, and everybody in the dugout practically fell over. I mean, everything the guy hits is on the barrel. Last year, he dropped off from .365 in 2009 to "only" .327. Just signed to a huge contract by the Minnesota Twins, Joe will be a mainstay in his hometown for years to come.

If Joe had a lick of speed, he might be our next .400 hitter.

WHAT'S THE HARDEST PITCH IN BASEBALL TO HIT?

I get asked that a lot during the Q & A sessions at the clinics I do.

Most people expect me to say something like a Mariano Rivera cutter or a Zack Greinke slider or a 100-mph Daniel Bard fastball.

My answer is always the same: the hardest pitch in baseball to hit is the *located* pitch.

Doesn't matter what it is—fastball, curve, slider, change, you name it. It's the pitch that the pitcher puts in exactly the place he knows the hitter has the toughest time getting to. For most hitters, that's down and away.

Hey, you think pitchers don't have scouting reports, too?

Proper mechanics are essential to learning to hit a baseball consistently and with authority. What I've tried to do in this chapter is to simplify as much as possible a complex process involving the entire body that must take place in the blink of an eye. Even if you've read this through twice, though, I don't expect you to be able to grab a bat and start hitting line drives to the gaps.

To do that, you need to go to the video—specifically, the video I mentioned earlier that Alex Rodriguez and I made together: *Pro Hitter's Workout* (www.championshipproductions.com). There you'll see in action in living color all the points I've made here, as demonstrated by one of the game's best hitters.

But you know what? I bet you still come away with the same conclusion that Ted Williams reached: hitting a baseball is the hardest thing to do in sport.

12 | A LONG DAY

Sunday afternoon in mid-August, second game of a makeup double-header against the White Sox, Chicago at its most sweltering. (Which is worse, the heat or the humidity? Who cares?)

We lose the first game 1–0 on a terrible call on a bang-bang play at home plate in the ninth inning. In the second game, we fall behind 3–0 early, and it stays that way through the eighth. Seems like all day long every guy in the lineup is swinging at bad pitches, lunging and flailing, getting fooled, taking called third strikes, generally looking like a Little Leaguer who's filling time until soccer season begins. Oh, well, at least we'll get out of Chicago at a halfway decent hour for our flight to Tampa Bay, where Tropicana Field has AC.

But in the top half of the ninth, two outs and everybody trying to forget this Sunday altogether, we load the bases on an error on an easy comebacker to the pitcher, a pop-up that drops between third and short for a single (one of those "I got it!"/"I got it!" deals where nobody gets it), and a terrible call on a 3–2 count that goes our way for a change. Next up, Alex Rodriguez. Alex is 0-for-7 on the day, but we all know that doesn't mean anything. As the man told us earlier in these pages, "Doesn't matter what you did your last time up or your last ten or your last thirty. Every time you go to the plate you're one good swing away from batting 1.000."

Crack! Just like that, Alex is batting 1.000, and we're up 4–3.

Man, all of us on the bench are thinking, at least we'll get out of Dodge with a split, and maybe even make it to Tampa Bay in good time. That thought lasts through two outs in the bottom of the ninth, when the White Sox tie it up on back-to-back-to-back bloop singles. (Yes, off Mariano. Never happens, but this night it did.) Five innings later, the Sox score on two walks and a single and, a little more than eleven hours after the first pitch of the day, we pile into a bus and head toward O'Hare.

At least we don't figure on running into any traffic.

(We didn't.)

Neither did we expect to sit on the runway for an hour as a hellacious midwestern thunderstorm that blew in off Lake Michigan stopped takeoffs and landings for an hour.

(We did.)

That falls under the heading of a long day, a *very* long day, wouldn't you agree? Well, it also falls under the heading of pure fiction: I made it up to make a point about how grueling a 162-game season can be. By mid-September, everybody's tail is dragging.

Now let me tell you about a really *Long* day, the kind that leaves me exhilarated no matter how long it takes to play, the kind I'd like to see 162 times a year. And this one is no fiction: it took place on August 19, 2010, in Yankee Stadium.

We went into our game against the Tigers that hot, sunny afternoon in a flat-footed tie with Tampa Bay for first place in the AL East. Detroit got off to a 2–0 lead in the first on a two-run shot by Miguel Cabrera, his thirty-first on the year. We came back to tie it in the fourth on singles by Tex, Swish, Robbie, and Grandy. And then, in the sixth, we scored nine big ones, with Robbie driving in three with a double and his twenty-fourth homer. *Nine* runs! Final score: Yankees 11, Tigers 5.

Even with all those runs, that game lasted only 2:56, just a shade above the major-league average (2:51 in 2010). But for me, it was a truly Long day.

But that only begins to describe a *full* Kevin Long day.

To make sure I didn't leave anything out, I asked my son Jaron to follow me around early in the summer of 2010 to help me record a typical Long day at Yankee Stadium. Jaron was eighteen at the time and had just finished high school in Scottsdale, where he was a good student and a terrific baseball player. More important for this assignment, he's an avid student of the game. I knew that he wouldn't miss a move. In fact, I knew he'd spot things that were so routine to me that I'd likely forget them if I tried to pull together one of my days from memory.

Jaron did a great job recording my every move. If you're like me, you get caught up in the workday and its complexities and later can't reconstruct its every detail later if your life depended on it. Jaron could help you with that.

Time Out!

Maybe now's as good a place as any to mention something you may have noticed if you're a student of the game (or just an intense fan, for that matter): namely, that I refer to myself throughout this book as a "hitting coach" even though my formal title with the Yankees is "batting coach."

How come? Well, it may not seem like much, but I want to help a guy hit, not just bat. Anybody can put a bat in his hands, stand up at the plate, and say, "Look, Ma! I'm batting." What I'm interested in is hitting, as in getting hits.

A distinction without a difference? I don't think so. I think there is *a big difference between just batting and hitting.*

Where was I before I so rudely interrupted myself? Oh, yes, giving you a running account of a typically long Kevin Long Day . . . specifically, the way it would roll out for a night game at Yankee Stadium.

1. Find a Starbucks. That's the easiest part of my day when we're playing at home. On the Upper East Side of Manhattan, where Marcey and I spend our summers, you're never more than a couple of blocks away from a Starbucks. Depending on the weather, I like to stretch myself and try a different location now and then, but one thing never varies: "Venti caramel macchiato with a triple shot, please." Now my day can begin.

2. Go to the subway station at Eighty-Sixth and Lexington. Pass through second turnstile entrance, go downstairs, take number 4 uptown train, get off ten minutes later at the 161st Street/River Avenue stop—Yankee Stadium.

3. Shoot to arrive at 12:30, no later than 1:00, for a 7:05 start. (Today, Jaron and I are there at 12:35.)

4. Walk through the Hard Rock Café, take elevator down, and enter our clubhouse.

5. Stick my head into Chad Bohling's office and give him grief about so-and-so going 0-for-4 last night against a pitcher he's supposed to own. Chad's our director of mental conditioning. Some of you older fans may be surprised to learn that most teams have someone on staff with a job title like that. Trust me: Chad's a huge plus. So naturally I like to rag on him when one of our guys doesn't live up to his coaching on attitude and mental preparation. He usually comes back with something like, "Maybe he needs a new hitting coach."

6. Next I swing by the kitchen to give a shout-out to Vic Rolden, our kitchen supervisor (someone you definitely want to stay on the good side of), and whatever other clubhouse staff guys are around. These guys work their butts off serving a bunch of picky-picky high-maintenance egos, and I think they can always use an extra tip of the cap.

7. Enter coaches' office; greet anybody who might have beaten me there. That doesn't happen often.

8. Check mail for any new announcements from on high or maybe an alteration to the travel schedule for our next road trip.

9. Put in my ticket requests for the day.

10. Get into my uni. From this point until the first pitch, my day's pretty hectic. That's why I shoot for that early arrival, 12:30–1:00, so that I'll have ample time to do the stuff I know I want to do and still have time to be able to respond to something I hadn't counted on, like a meeting Brian Cashman might call to talk about a player who's not performing up to par. I give Cash shit all the time about everything, but we all want to be on the same page when it comes to our players. He always tells me that these meetings wouldn't be necessary if I was doing my job.

11. From spring training up until about the All-Star break, I spend my first hour at the Stadium in our fitness room doing thirty minutes of cardio on the bike or the treadmill and forty-five minutes or so of upper body. That's right: mostly upper body. Beach muscle workout! But as the season progresses, those workouts are the first thing to go.

12. Meet with Joe Girardi and third-base coach Rob Thomson to talk about the day's lineup. No surprises, usually. Maybe I'll say that a certain guy could use an off day. Or maybe Rob will suggest that we work in a kid we've just called up, the idea being the longer he sits around waiting, the more pressure he's going to put on himself. Joe makes the final call, of course.

13. Get my pitcher cards and game charts ready and head down to our video room. Each pitcher card is drawn from data that I've pulled together on how a guy's done in the past against us and opposing teams. These cards give our players basic info that'll help them know what to expect from the pitchers we'll be facing.

14. The game charts put together by Charlie "Super Scout" Wonsowicz measure a player's quality at bats, hard-hit balls, chases out of the zone, walks/plate appearances' percentage, and whether with a runner on second and no outs (R2 0-Out) he advanced the guy to third or not. Runner on third less than two outs (R3< 2-Out), did he get him in or not? Number of pitches seen per at bat? Number of walks? I use this chart to keep our hitters aware and accountable for what they do, and I update the charts throughout the season. If a player's struggling, his chart helps me determine whether the problem has to do with mechanics, approach, strike zone discipline, or whatever.

15. Beginning at about 1:30, if things have gone smoothly since I got to the ballpark, I start watching video on pitchers two, three, or maybe even four series down the road. My inventory on opposing pitchers in the league is very good now, but there are still new pitchers on every team whom I need to add. A key part of my job is to keep careful tabs on the pitchers we're likely to face and write an up-to-the-minute report on each of them.

16. Each opposing pitcher I review gets his own card. I start with the obvious—name, team, uniform number, lefty or righty—and then move quickly on to the nitty gritty. First, his stuff: FB, CB, SL, CH, SPL, KN, CT—fastball, curveball, slider, change, split finger, knuckler, cutter—with his velocity range for each. (Example: FB 88–93.) Then a note on the action on each of his pitches. (Example: "SL tight with good down action . . . not much side action or sweep . . . small to medium depth.") Then the usage percentage of each pitch to both righty and lefty batters. (Example: FB 63%; CB 7%; SL 18%; CH 12% to RHs.)

17. Next I assess a pitcher's control and command of his stuff. Some pitchers have pinpoint control; others are very inconsistent. Some have good control of one pitch, but not so much on any of their other pitches. It's my job to sort through this stuff and relay it to our hitters. I also check to see if a guy uses his slider or maybe his changeup more with runners in scoring position. If that's the case, we've found his out-pitch.

18. Finally, I write a brief summary on each pitcher. Here's a sample: "Low ¾ arm slot . . . Good arm and stuff . . . Attacks hitters with good two-seam FB with SL as second pitch . . . Very inconsistent with command of all his pitches . . . Will leave pitches in the middle of the plate . . . FB has good run with slight sink. Has trouble commanding to cross arm side of plate . . . SL is small with just bigger than cutter action, does have small depth." (Sound like gibberish? Not to my guys.) Then comes a brief summary of how the guy comes at right-handed hitters and left-handed hitters. All that stuff goes to Steve Martone, who keyboards everything into the computer base, after which he prints out a report on 8½" x 11" sheets of card stock. Bingo! A pitcher card!

19. Once I'm done reviewing opposing pitchers for the next two or three upcoming series, I "re-review" the starter we're facing that night. I do this to see if he is doing anything different and also to refresh my memory. I'll also look briefly at the main guys in the other team's bullpen.

20. My final pregame focus is on our hitters. I analyze who's hot, who's not, who's *really* struggling. Then I focus on what I can do to help them. (The first category's easy: I just stay out of their way.) For the other two groups, I usually look at video and try to detect something that may not be quite right with either their setup, their hands, their load, their use of their lower half, and so on. If I spot something a little off, I'll generally address it with the player later. (I don't want him to go up to the plate thinking "Adjustment! Adjustment!" without our having worked on it.)

Usually, I'll pull up video from when guys were hot and compare it with recent video showing them struggling. This is where I must determine the source of his current problem and whether it can be addressed with a little drill work. Sometimes it's as simple as body fatigue, and I'll suggest to Joe that a day off might help.

21. *Gentlemen, let's go to the cage.* Once I've completed my overall review, it's time for cage work back under the stands. With only an occasional exception, usually related to a minor injury, my hitters visit the cage every day before a game. My job is to monitor them carefully, always looking for something tiny that's crept into a swing that can be eliminated before it becomes a big problem. Each hitter has his own set of drills. As I said, when a hitter's going good, there's not much to discuss. If a player's been struggling, I'll usually go over a point or two I'd like to see him focus on before he steps up to the plate. I keep everything low-key, casual. This is pregame prep for a regular-season ball game, not the last half of the ninth in Game 7 of the World Series.

22. Next stop, BP on the field. This is standard with every team in baseball. Early-arriving fans get to watch players hit screaming liners and long homers off coaches throwing 60-mph fastballs right down the middle. Fun to watch, but not all that revealing. We have five batting practice throwers: Tony Peña, Mick Kelleher, Brett Weber, Mike Harkey, and myself. Our only job is to throw strikes. The guys loosening up against us take care of the rest.

23. My job during BP, when I'm not getting my best stuff knocked off the outfield walls, is to help Rob Thomson, the coach in charge of BP, make everything run smoothly and on time. I usually stand on the safe side of the screen right behind them and watch guys take their cuts. Often I'll give them game situations—"Man on third, one out" or "First and third, nobody out"—but only rarely do I try to "teach" a guy anything during BP. I might make a mental note of something I'll want to raise the next time he's

doing cage work back in my office, but never do I suggest he try something new or different. Wrong time, wrong place. My guys know the turtle cage is for loosening up, getting the groove of going the other way, hitting line drives, and going over their mechanics checklists.

24. After BP, at about 5:30, I grab a quick bite to eat. God, am I ravenous!

25. If it's the first game of a series, we have a fifteen-minute advance meeting in the clubhouse—Thoms, Killer, me, and all the position players (except for those getting worked on in the trainer's room). If it's the second half of the season, and we've played our opponents recently, Joe usually scratches this meeting. If we do have it, I usually just give our guys a brief rundown on their starters and how they use their bullpen. If they have any new faces on their staff—say, somebody recently brought up from the minors—I need to have the skinny on them, too. These meetings are short and to the point.

26. About half of the starters head back to the cage for a few more swings. Why so many swings? Muscle memory and feel are crucial to all hitters, and guys like Derek, A-Rod, Swish, and Gardy believe those few extra swings bring them to just where they want to be before the home plate ump yells "Play ball!"

27. Head to the dugout and get ready for the fun. My pregame ritual starts with me taking a seat on the bat rack. About five minutes before game time, I rattle all the bats to "wake them up." Then I throw Jorge Posada's gamers out of the rack and yell at them: "Wake up *now!*" I get pretty fired up during this whole act. The guys love it. So do I.

28. 7:05 P.M. This is the best part of my day, one that began at Starbucks eight hours ago and won't be finished for another three or so. I have my pitcher cards. I have my chart. I'm ready.

29. During the game I'll give verbal reminders about the stuff and tendencies of the pitcher who's on the mound against us. D.J.

will kick it off by shouting down the bench, "K-Long! Who's this guy?" I'll yell back the pitcher's name, and he'll holler, "I don't know him! What's he got?" Usually that's bullshit; D.J. may have faced the guy a hundred or more times. But he likes to pull my chain, so I rattle off what the guy throws, how fast his fastball is, and if it's straight or not. This may help Jeter or not—as I said, he's been around the horn in the league, and he has a lock-trap memory—but I think it helps get everybody else focused, and I'm delighted for D.J. to put me on the spot.

30. When we're up, I take my spot at the end of the dugout nearest home plate right next to Joe. This is the closest I can get to the hitter, and the best position from which to remind guys of things as they go to the on-deck circle. As relief pitchers come into the game, our guys will often come over and get a quick rundown on the new pitcher. By the time they're on deck, they've been informed and are ready to go.

31. There in the dugout when we're up, I keep my own stats for each of our hitters on three things: hard-hit balls, chases out of the strike zone, and quality at bats. I also compile detailed notes on every pitcher we see that day for later use in putting together my "pitcher cards."

32. When we're in the field, I head straight back to Anthony Flynn's video room and analyze the swings I've just seen live. Many times a guy will ask me about the swing or the pitch location during his last at bat, and I need to be ready to give him quick, precise feedback. Like all other coaches and managers, I get a real rush when an in-game adjustment, however small, helps win a ball game.

33. Yankees win!

A long day, wouldn't you agree?

It's pretty much the same drill for 1:05 P.M. starts, except that I have to get up at the crack of dawn to make it to the Stadium by 8:30–9:00. (Good thing Starbucks opens at 6:00 A.M.) On the road, of course, I don't have access to our video library, and the cage we use for pregame work is nothing like what we have back in New York. But I still try to be the first one to arrive at the park. Who knows, one of my guys might want to get in a little extra work.

So every game day is a long day, whether it's a day or night game, at home or on the road—and that's without factoring in extra innings.

But hey, you know what? Anytime the Yankees come out on top, that long day is also a *Long* day.

13 | MEET THE *OTHER* A-TEAM

Baseball fans already know about A-Rod, D.J., Robbie, Swish, Tex, Mariano, C.C., Jorge, and the other guys who do it on the field for the Yankees. But there's another group of guys in the Yankees clubhouse who don't blast game-winning home runs or throw 93-mph cutters to close out games, but who do have a huge impact on the W-L column.

Let me start at the top.

JOE GIRARDI

Joe's a great communicator. In New York, considering that after some games in Yankee Stadium the civilians with notepads and microphones and minicams outnumber the players in the clubhouse, any manager of the Yankees who wants to stay in pinstripes better be great with the media. Joe's super about it. He doesn't toot his own horn; he doesn't dodge tough questions; he doesn't play favorites; he doesn't try to shift responsibility; he doesn't bad-mouth his players; and he doesn't lie. Not ever.

What he *does* do is credit his players and, if need be, defend them.

To a man, the coaches on our staff respect him. When he talks with us, he's not just going through the motions: the man genuinely wants our input. He makes us feel important, treats all of us like we're members of his immediate family—which, for at least eight months of the year, we are. After all, he sees us more from March through October than he sees his wife, Kim, and their three kids, Serena, Dante, and Lena.

Joe looks you in the eye and asks specific, concrete questions, not a lot of meaningless "Howzit goin'?" bullshit. Most important, Joe *listens*. In my book, that's the key to being a great communicator. Trust me, from what I've picked up in my four years in the majors, Joe's interaction with his coaches isn't even close to being universal among major-league managers.

The man had a solid fifteen-season major-league career as a catcher for four teams, including four years with the Yankees (1996–1999), two as a starter and two as Jorge Posada's backup. Before taking over the Yankees in 2008, Joe had just one season as a big-league manager under his belt, but it was a doozy. That was in 2006, when he led the Marlins to a 78–84 season. Sounds shabby, but the Marlins were loaded with rookies, and Joe kept them in contention late into the summer. The Baseball Writers Association of America named Joe Girardi 2006 NL Manager of the Year.

In 2009, in just his second year with the Yankees, Joe joined a very select club when he became only the third Yankee—Ralph Houk and Billy Martin were the others—to play for *and* manage World Championship teams. Joe won his first three World Series rings as a player in 1996, 1998, and 1999, and his fourth as our manager in 2009.

The way Joe treats the people around him reminds me of Coach D back in my days at Thunderbird High. It's an approach I've tried to use since my first day as a coach. Fans just looking at Joe in the dugout or listening to him giving postgame sound bites on TV can't be expected to see that side of him, but let me tell you, when it comes to communicating with his people and making us feel like he really, truly cares about us, Joe Girardi is a Hall of Famer.

If you can't tell the players without a scorecard, what about the coaches?

Here's my challenge for you: excluding your own team, name five coaches—*coaches,* not managers—in the major leagues. Give up? I thought so, but that's perfectly okay. We're not the reason die-hard Yankees fans plunk down anywhere from $20 for a seat in the last row of the upper deck in deep right, to $300 for a field-level box between the bases in Yankee Stadium—a whole lot more if the Red Sox are in town and they have to scalp. But coaches do play an important role in a team's success or failure, so let me introduce, in alphabetical order (with their first season in their present job in parentheses), my colleagues on the 2011 Yankees coaching staff.

P.S.: I'm doing it in alphabetical order and I'm giving everybody as close as I can manage equal time so that nobody gives me grief once this comes out. (Fat chance that'll work out.)

MIKE HARKEY, BULLPEN COACH (2008)

Hark's job is to make sure that guys coming into a game are mentally prepared for the batters they'll be facing. Yes, they're all major leaguers, and they all go to the advance meeting before a series, but mental preparation is so important in this game that another quick review of where a certain hitter likes the ball just may give a relief pitcher getting ready to take the ball a slight edge. Or at least give him the feeling that he has one, which can be just as important in this little head game we coach.

At six-foot-seven and about 260 pounds, Mike Harkey is one seriously large human being, especially from my perspective, which is about a foot closer to the ground than his. (Fans are all the time mistaking him for C. C. Sabathia.) Hark worked for Joe as bullpen coach for the Marlins in 2006, and when Joe took over the Yankees in 2008, Hark was one of his first hires.

You won't find it on our résumés, but Hark and I head up a little-known basketball dynasty in Florida. Every spring training since Hark came on board three years ago, a team composed of (NY, American League) Yankees coaches and front office personnel has consistently shellacked a team composed of (Tampa, Florida State League) Yankees coaches and front office personnel. We try to play three or four times during spring training, full-court games that leave us crawling back to the showers. Hark's got bad pins and spends almost as much time getting ice and having a trainer work on his legs as he does on the court. We're both forty-four, and we've sworn that 2011 will be our last year of basketball.

But come 2012, who knows? We just might stage a mighty comeback.

MICK KELLEHER, FIRST-BASE COACH (2009)

One of the all-time nicest guys you'll ever meet. Really, not a bad bone in him. I swear the man has the sunniest disposition of anybody I've ever worked with. We could be on a ten-game losing streak—just talking hypothetically here; the longest losing streak since I've been a Yankee was seven games (in April 2007)—and Killer would be throwing off a positive vibe.

In an eleven-season big-league career, Killer played short, second, and third with five teams (Cardinals, Astros, Cubs, Tigers, Angels). He wasn't exactly known for his bat—lifetime .213 BA—but he was a *superior* glove man. After his retirement as a player in 1982, Killer's baseball savvy earned him hitches over the years as a roving minor-league infield instructor or defensive coordinator for four clubs (Padres, Cubs, Brewers, Yankees). He also had stints in the majors as first-base coach and infield instructor for the Pirates (1986) and the Tigers (2003–2005).

For us, Killer mans the first-base box but also carries a second title more in line with his real expertise: infield instructor.

Every coaching staff should be so lucky to have a guy like Mick around. Need a good bottle of wine? Talk to Killer, he knows his cabs. Need a smile to lift your spirits? Go find Killer. And on top of that, Marcey swears that his wife, Renée, is even nicer than her husband.

Killer's also the answer to a pretty good baseball trivia question: What major-league position player in the last three decades retired with the most at bats without a home run? That's right! Mick Kelleher: 0-for-1,081.

(Sorry, Killer. I just had to get that in.)

KEVIN LONG, HITTING COACH (2007)

Never heard of him.

TONY PEÑA, BENCH COACH (2009)

Pancho or Panchito, as he's known around the clubhouse, is a savvy baseball man and a wonderfully warm human being. Tony is an ageless wonder (actually, he's a young fifty-three) who brings a knapsack full of energy with him every day he comes to work.

A five-time National League All-Star catcher, Panchito posted a .260 career batting average and won four Gold Gloves over his eighteen-year major-league career with six teams (Pirates, Cardinals, Red Sox, Indians, White Sox, Astros). He ranks fifth all-time among major-league catchers with 1,950 games behind the plate, trailing only Ivan Rodriguez, Carlton Fisk, Bob Boone, and Gary Carter. Born in the Dominican Republic, Tony didn't play high school baseball; he says his mother, an outstanding softball player, taught him how to play the game.

Panchito throws Group 1 of batting practice before every game and is, without doubt, the best BP pitcher I've ever seen. "Best" among BP pitchers, by the way, is the guy who throws the most 60-mph fastballs for strikes; work the corners, get cute with your cutter, or throw something nasty low and away and you're sure to catch hell from the batters. That pinpoint control shouldn't come as a surprise, considering that over his major-league career, Tony threw out 35 percent of runners trying to steal.

It's an old (and true) baseball axiom that baserunners steal on the pitcher and get thrown out by the catcher, so it's a relevant factoid that in 2009, Yankees catchers caught a major-league-best 167 potential base stealers. Guess which Yankees coach doubles up as catching instructor? Stand up and take a bow, Panchito.

Joe made Tony his bench coach in 2009, bringing him in from the first-base coaching box, where he'd served since 2006. Before that, Panchito had managed the Royals. In his first full season with KC (2003), he won AL Manager of the Year honors for leading the Royals to an 83–79 record from a 62–100 flop the year before. That gives us *two* ex–Managers of the Year in our dugout. Nice to know that if your manager gets tossed for arguing a terrible call that you have an experienced, first-rate replacement standing by.

If there were a Shoppers Hall of Fame, Tony Peña would be a first-ballot shoo-in. This guy can shop like no one I've ever seen, and that includes Marcey. To kill time on road trips before going to the ballpark, I've often gone mall wandering with Tony only to come back to our hotel with four bags of clothing I didn't need (and gifts for Marcey and my kids that they don't need) and about a grand missing from my wallet. His passion is contagious—and dangerous. The man's got great taste, but I swear he's never seen a deal he didn't like.

LARRY ROTHSCHILD, PITCHING COACH (2011)

The basic approaches of a pitching coach and a hitting coach are pretty much the same: keep your guys on track, keep a sharp eye out for any negative changes that slip in, and keep their spirits up when they're going through a rough patch.

But when one of my guys starts pulling ofers, he's got eight teammates who want to pick him up. When a pitcher goes south, he's all alone out there. The only way to "pick him up" is to get him out of the game. One of my guys gets a slight muscle strain, he can maybe DH until he gets better. If a pitcher suffers the same thing, he's got to sit until he's 100 percent (or almost) for fear of damaging his most valuable commodity: his arm.

No doubt about it—a pitching coach's job is super demanding.

(Let me call a brief timeout to tip my cap to Dave Eiland, who was our pitching coach from 2008 through 2010. Dave's a gutsy guy: he pitched in the majors for the Yankees, Padres, and Rays in a ten-year career that included two Tommy John surgeries. I know our pitchers benefited from his experience and insights.)

The rookie on our coaching staff is a guy who's been around major-league baseball since Abner Doubleday. Well, almost. Entering the 2011 season, Larry Rothschild had been in professional baseball "only" thirty-six years.

A right-handed pitcher, Larry was signed by the Reds in 1975 and made it to the majors with the Tigers for a short visit (1981–82). Most recently (2002–10), Larry was pitching coach of the Chicago Cubs. Over that span, his staff led the majors in strikeouts. Larry has two World Series rings, earned when he was bullpen coach for the 1990 Reds and pitching coach for the 1997 Marlins. He was the Rays' first manager (1998–2001) before joining the Cubs.

Larry's from the "other" league, so I don't know him well, but I'm looking forward to working with him.

ROB THOMSON, THIRD-BASE COACH (2008)

Thoms is the hardest-working guy in baseball. He's our general manager in uniform. He organizes everything from schedules, to lineup cards, to

BP times, to spray charts, to clubhouse meetings, to . . . well, just about every one of those i's and t's that have to be dotted and crossed if you want your outfit to run like a well-oiled machine.

On top of that, Thoms is an unbelievable third-base coach, not an easy job because of the split-second decisions that have to be made on whether to send a guy home or not. A lot of fans don't realize how much a good third-base coach like Rob can help a club. Last summer, when Whitey Herzog was inaugurated into the Hall of Fame, the *New York Times* quoted an old (1966) story in which Whitey talked about his own days coaching at the hot corner:

> A good third-base coach can win 16 or 17 games a season for his club. When a base runner has a chance to score, you've got to remember that the percentage is with him. It's like being a gambler—you'll force the other side to make either a perfect play or a damaging mistake. [Casey Stengel taught me] that good base running boils down to anticipation and knowledge of the defense . . . You can steal a lot of runs.

Thoms makes great decisions on the fly. Rarely ever do you find yourself shaking your head and thinking to yourself, *Damn! He should have stopped him/sent him!* And when Rob does blow one, something he does about twice a summer, max, he also blows a gasket. A perfectionist in everything he does, the man goes off on himself when he sends a runner home with no outs and the guy gets thrown out.

The thing I like best about having Rob Thomson in the third-base box for us is his aggressiveness. Some 3B coaches will cover their asses by holding runners unless they're absolutely sure they can score. Not Rob. No doubt in part because he knows we're capable of scoring a lot of runs—we led the majors with 915 in our 2009 championship season—but mainly because he's a balls-out kind of guy, Thoms will wave on runners that a lot of other coaches would throw up the stop sign to.

For instance, in the fifth inning of a Saturday day game against the Blue Jays in the Stadium in the summer of 2010, Nick Swisher was out trying to score from first base on a double by Mark Teixeira, and in the very next at bat Tex was nailed at home by a great throw from DeWayne Wise after a long fly-out to center by A-Rod. That's right—*two* guys thrown out at home in one inning.

So after the game, when reporters cornered him in the clubhouse, did Rob blame himself or the umps or guys not hustling or mysterious forces of nature? No way. "Hey, give them credit," Rob said. "They made two perfect throws from 408 feet away. You tip your cap and move on."

Of course, Thoms's calm, generous "It's all part of the game" response may have been affected by the fact that we won, 7–6, in ten innings. If we'd lost, he'd have been kicking his own ass pretty hard.

Thoms also runs our spring training camp down in Tampa. Talk about your logistical nightmare! We're lucky. Perfectionist that he is, General Thomson makes sure that everybody's in the right place at the right time doing the right thing. That makes getting ready for the season go a lot smoother.

A man who knows the importance of good food, especially on the road, Rob can also tell you where to get the best wings on the planet— that would be Hooters, in case you're planning a trip anytime soon.

ALSO STARRING . . .

We also have a support staff of guys around the clubhouse who contribute a lot but never get any curtain calls. **Brett Weber** operates our radar gun, charts pitches, throws BP, and helps out in the cages. A Yankee for eleven years, **Roman Rodriguez** helps throw BP and warms up Mariano & Co. in the bullpen. For the last six seasons, **Chad Bohling** has been our "attitude coach." Massage therapist **Doug Cecil** will begin his first year with the Yankees in 2011. **Ben Tuliebitz** has been our traveling secretary since I started coaching and is someone I rely on heavily every year. **Jason Zillo** does a tremendous job helping all of us with the media. **Anthony Flynn** moved up to become video coordinator in 2010 and has brought new levels of sarcastic wit and state-of-the-art rags to that department. Our strength and conditioning coordinator, **Dana Cavalea,** works his tail off working our players' tails off to keep them strong and in shape. **Rob Cucuzza** and his brother **Lou** are our home and visiting clubhouse managers; they've been running Yankees clubhouses for longer than some of our players are old.

Like so much else about the Yankees, those guys are the best in the business.

AND NOW, LAST BUT NOT LEAST . . .
CHARLIE "SUPER SCOUT" WONSOWICZ

To me, for all the help he gave me my first four seasons with the Yankees, this guy is the unsung superstar of our little band of brothers.

Charlie *who?*

Yeah, I know, nobody outside the Yankees family (and his own) could identify the behind-the-scenes genius of our club. A Yankee for almost twenty years now, "The Great Wonz" (as he sometimes calls himself) started as a lefty BP thrower and moved on to charting pitches and working the radar gun. But Wonz made his mark with the team as video guru and analyst for fifteen seasons.

That's sort of like saying Michael Jordan played basketball for fifteen seasons in the NBA and stopping there. Charlie's a wonder. Drawing on our incredible video library (every pitch, every swing of every Yankee over the past fifteen years) and his own computer mastery, Charlie put together the scouting reports that I depended on to do my job my first three years with the club. If I wanted to know how Derek Jeter hit left-handers on odd-numbered days when the temperature was 68–76 degrees, all I had to do was ask Wonz.

The biggest reason our five-monitor video room next to our club-house in Yankee Stadium is typically SRO before games is because of Charlie Wonz's skill in teaching our players how to tap into this hugely valuable scouting resource. During games, some guys, if they make an out, go straight down to the video room about five seconds later to look at the at bat. A lot of our pitchers spend time in the video room checking their deliveries and scouting opposing hitters.

(Another attraction of our video room, especially during New York's sweltering hot summer of 2010: AC.)

Now our top in-house scout, Wonz passed on day-to-day management of the video library to his protégé, Anthony Flynn, at the beginning of 2010. Tough act to follow, but Flynnie's not missed a beat.

We take our video gear with us on road trips, and Flynnie finds a place in each clubhouse to set up, and we're in business. Not as good as the setup we have in the Stadium, but it's okay.

But let's go back to Super Scout, whose pitching reports helped me more in 2009 in the development of my game plans than anything else. Charlie helped organize me and took the pitching charts to another level. I've always put together the actual reports and individual cards on each pitcher. When information on a certain pitcher was wrong, we usually blamed Wonz in good fun, but it really fell on me. If I'd say a pitcher is doing *this* and one of my hitters said he thought the guy was doing *that*, all we had to do was go speak to Charlie and—*presto!*—my guy learned that I hadn't been blowing smoke.

Thanks, Wonz.

Now Coming to the Plate, Marcey Long

During spring training in 2009, with two full years under our belts as official members of the Yankees family, Kevin and I bonded with some other members of that big family: the Zillos

(Jason is the director of media relations), the Thomsons, the Kellehers, and the Wonsowiczes. Picnics at the pool, margarita madness after games, Michele Thomson's great home cooking, and our morning meetings at Starbucks brought us close together.

Then on to New York!

That summer, Mick, Rob, and Kev lived at On the Ave, a "boutique" hotel on the Upper West Side. After two years in an Upper East Side apartment, I thought this was going to be a disaster. Hotel living? Been there, done that.

Boy, was I wrong. We girls had a blast. The lobby at On the Ave was our gathering place where we decided what to do with our days (and evenings!). Blondies Sports Bar on Seventy-Ninth Street between Broadway and Amsterdam figured regularly in those plans. The owners, Jill and Patty, were so generous to us, and we'll never forget Ken, our favorite bartender.

Evenings when we weren't at Blondies or a ball game I spent going to just about every Broadway and off-Broadway show in town. My favorites? Well, I loved Wicked, *but* Lion King *reminded me of when the kids were growing up and the Disney movie and the sound track were big hits in our household.*

Many of my days I spent serving as tour guide for any visitors we might have in town, which was pretty much every day all summer long.

And none *of my time was spent making beds, pushing a vacuum cleaner, or doing laundry!*

Hotel living? Not so bad after all!

A strong crew, take my word for it. No weak links, I promise you, present company included. True, we haven't been together as a unit all that long. But we have a lot of fun together, and we work well together, and I know those two things are related.

Now let me close with an observation that won't be exactly hot news to Yankees lovers *or* Yankees haters: in my completely objective opinion, the New York Yankees organization, top to bottom, is absolutely top-drawer, the very best in baseball.

14 | PLEASED TO MEET YOU, MR. PRESIDENT

Our 2009 World Championship season didn't come to an official end until a little over three weeks into the 2010 season when, on April 26, the whole team crammed into the East Wing of the White House to meet and shake hands with President Barack Obama.

That morning, we had visited the Walter Reed Medical Center to meet with some of our wounded veterans of the wars in Iraq and Afghanistan. Man, that visit put things in perspective for me. We all say we appreciate the sacrifices our men and women in the armed services make on our country's behalf, but when you meet them face-to-face in wheelchairs and hospital beds, some of them missing parts of their bodies, it really, really drives home how much we owe them. From their smiles and the happiness in their eyes, I know that they were genuinely glad to see us—even the ones who wore their Red Sox caps!

This visit to the White House was, needless to say, a whole bunch different from the year before when I toured it with some of our players and coaches on an off day before a series with the Orioles. This time, I got to meet the president of the United States—and shake his hand!

I was a little surprised to find that the president is taller than he looks on TV. Just as lean as he looks on the tube, but taller. Maybe that's why his game is basketball. (Shooting guard? Maybe. But I see him at point guard, running the offense.) What I was most impressed with was how at ease he was, how casual and open and direct. Shouldn't be surprised, of course—the man's made a few speeches in his career, all of them a lot tougher than the short one he had to give to us.

A longtime White Sox fan, President Obama reminded us that not so long ago *his* team had been where we were this day: "I remember 2005, so don't get too comfortable." Naturally, he took the opportunity to take a little shot at that "other" team in Chicago: "It's nine years since your last title, which must have seemed like an eternity . . . Some teams would love a spell like that, a team like the Cubs, for instance." He also tipped his hat in Mo's direction: "For a White Sox fan like me, it's painful to watch Mariano's cutter." But the thing that touched me the most was when he said that Derek Jeter, our captain, "epitomizes the best of the Yankees tradition." Truer words were never spoken.

At the end of the ceremony, Joe Girardi presented the president with a Yankees home uni top with the number 27 on the back. Joe didn't have to explain to President Obama what the number signified.

What a great way to spend an off day!

The 2009 season began on September 30, 2008. We'd just finished with a winning record (89–73), but so had three other teams in the AL East, by far the best in baseball that year. For us, the key numbers were 8, 6, 3, as in *eight games* behind the Rays, *six games* behind the Red Sox, and *third place* in the AL East. We ended the season September 29 with, fittingly enough, a 4–3 loss in Fenway Park. No October baseball for the New York Yankees.

Not good enough. Not close to good enough for anyone wearing pinstripes. Not good enough for the 4.3 million fans who came out to cheer us on at Yankee Stadium that year, or the millions more who watched us come up short on TV. The New York Yankees are supposed to still be playing baseball when autumn leaves start to fall, not back home raking them up.

So you guys needed a total overhaul, right? No, not close, at least not in my department. We needed pitching. We finished eighth in the AL in ERA, and our horse, Mike Mussina, had announced his retirement on a 20–9, 3.37 high note. But everybody knew Brian Cashman would bust his ass over the winter doing something about that. And our hitting core was rock solid: Alex and Derek, Johnny Damon, Hideki Matsui and Melky Cabrera, and Robinson Cano, plus Jorge Posada coming back from rotator cuff surgery on his throwing shoulder that limited him to just 195 at bats in 2008. To a man, we believed we could do a lot better, *would* do a lot better, in 2009. And you know what? We did. We were able to stay healthy, and that made a *huge* difference.

Now Coming to the Plate, Marcey Long

At the end of the 2008 season, when we finished third in the AL East, I knew Kevin would return home an unhappy guy. After getting settled back into the rhythm of off-season living—always an adjustment for all involved, including our little Yorkie, Madeline Elizabeth—we sat down to discuss what we were going to do that winter. And I knew what was coming: "Babe, I don't think we'll be doing much traveling like we'd hoped to. I mean, I feel like I've got to be available to see as many players as I can squeeze in. I hope you understand."

Did I understand? If I had learned one thing in eighteen years of marriage to this man, it was that he is superdedicated to doing the best job he possibly can. And part of my job is to make it as easy as possible for him to do just that.

I should have had T-shirts made up for him: "Have Bat, Will Travel!"

The day after the final out of the 2008 season, I already knew what my number one off-season project was going to be: Robinson Cano.

Then just twenty-five years old, Cano had finished his fourth year as our second baseman on a down note, at least compared with what he'd shown his first three years on the job:

YR	BA	HR	RBI	OBP
2005	.297	14	62	.320
2006	.342	15	78	.365
2007	.306	19	97	.353
2008	.271	14	72	.305

Most second basemen in baseball (not to mention their managers) would be delighted with numbers like that, but here's the bottom line on Robinson Cano's 2008 season: he *under*achieved.

Robbie and I first hooked up in 2004 after he'd earned a midseason promotion to Columbus, and our relationship continued through the following spring training and into the first month of the 2005 season, when he was called up to the Yankees. (Smart move by Brian Cashman. Robbie finished second in the Rookie of the Year voting that season behind Oakland reliever Huston Street.)

Robbie Cano is special. I've watched him grow and develop and mature and begin to understand how good he can be if he stays focused and continues to work hard. Too many guys I've seen with a lot of natural talent think that's enough, that they can get by with the skills that have set them apart since they were kids. Not Robbie. He really cares about the game, really cares about the Yankees. He knows there aren't any shortcuts. Fortunately, he has some great role models to guide him: D.J., Jorge, Tex, A-Rod.

But 2008 had definitely been an "off" year for Robbie, so I suggested to him that maybe it'd be a good idea if I came down to the Dominican Republic in early January so we could work on a few things. He was delighted. Not a surprising reaction on his part, considering how dedicated he is to improving his game and becoming more consistent. For me, it was a no-brainer because I so respect that kind of attitude, and because I knew going there and working with him would make the Yankees a better team. Hey, I had two seasons in pinstripes under my belt, but I still hadn't tasted a World Championship.

The hard part would be leaving my family and heading to the Dominican Republic in the middle of my winter "vacation." I kept reminding myself of the sacrifices it would take on everyone's part for me to do my job the way I believed in my heart it needed to be done. A lot of those sacrifices would be made by my family.

Here I was, just twelve days after my forty-second birthday, taking my first trip ever (not counting road trips to Toronto) out of the United States! To the baseball factory known as the Dominican Republic! Boy, was I psyched!

Robbie originally booked me into a suite at a fancy resort near Santo Domingo. His plan was to drive in from his home in San Pedro de Macorís every day and take me back to his hometown where we would do our work. Nice gesture, but I was more interested in spending time with him and his family in San Pedro. No problem. Robbie got me a hotel room at the Embassy Suites, fifteen minutes from where he lived. Great move. If we hadn't made the change, I wouldn't have been able to enjoy the delicious cooking of Robbie's mother, Claribel.

There've been a ton of mighty fine ballplayers who grew up in San Pedro—Tony Fernandez, Sammy Sosa, George Bell, Rico Carty, Pedro Guerrero, Juan Samuel, and Mariano Duncan, to name just a few—but let me assure you that right now, today, Robinson Cano is *El Hombre*.

(And yes, as you probably already know, he was named after a great Hall of Fame second baseman—Jackie Robinson.)

I love the Dominican Republic.

Sure, the poverty, compared with anything I'd ever known or seen before in my life, was staggering. But even more staggering was the warmth and generosity of the people I met there. All of them, from Robbie's friends and family to total strangers, were completely welcoming to this awestruck gringo who didn't speak a word of their language beyond *una cerveza, por favor*.

Yet as much as I wished I could travel around more and get to know the place better, I was there to work, and we got right down to it.

We started with Robbie's base, as I always do with everybody, because in my book that's where all good things in hitting a baseball begin. We squared his stance up and got him into a better and more consistent position to see and attack the baseball. We talked about working hard, and then working some more. We talked about getting into shape and staying that way, no matter what the calendar said.

If Robbie Cano has a flaw in his mental makeup when he goes to the plate, it's that he likes to jump on anything that looks good. A smart pitcher with good command who understands that about Robbie's eagerness can sometimes get him to chase *his* pitch. Robbie knows he has to work on being more selective. If he doesn't, he also knows I'll be on him like white on rice. And his .305 OBP in 2008 was just plain unacceptable. So we talked a lot about being more patient at the plate, about being willing to take a first strike, about making sure he got something he could drive.

Part of his challenge to being more selective was simply the fact that he'd been in the big leagues only four years. A lot of young guys are like that; they go up there hacking at everything. They're long on talent but short on patience. I tell my younger guys over and over, "You're only as good as the pitches you swing at. If you swing at balls outside the zone, you will never tap your full potential." I don't have to tell the veterans that; they already know it.

As to his mechanics, Robbie has a slight drift to his swing that I monitor every time he goes to the plate and that we work on all the time. By "drift" I mean a movement forward to his front side. Not normally something I'm too thrilled with, but I'm okay with "slight," at least for Robbie. At six feet and 205 pounds, he's solidly built and has great power for a middle infielder—25 home runs in 2009, 29 in 2010—with the potential to be a consistent 30-HR guy.

But Robbie occasionally gets into trouble. When he's looking fastball and gets something off-speed, he sometimes jumps out too much on his right side. How much is too much? In Robbie's case, sliding forward twelve inches instead of the six to eight inches we shoot for in the cage can make a dramatic difference. Doesn't sound like much, does it? Believe me, it is. We're talking about the hardest thing to do in sport, remember, where "little" things like a few inches mean the difference between journeyman and All-Star.

We worked hard those five days in San Pedro de Macorís, and Robbie was amped up to start winter ball for his home team and try some of the stuff we'd been working on. The Yankees had agreed to let him DH in winter ball, but absolutely no playing in the field; no way were we going to risk losing him to a bad knee injury from a collision at second on a DP. There was a buzz throughout the city that first night he was set to play for the first time. We'd gone to a game a few days earlier, and the stands were half empty. Not on this night. The place was jumping with excitement, all because hometown hero Robbie Cano was starting at DH. Robbie was excited and fired up to play; he really wanted to help his team, at that time in last place, to win some games. That night he went 1-for-5 with 2 RBIs, and I was thankful to file away another experience I'll never forget.

I like to think our little visit together in January paid some big dividends back in New York that year, when Robbie's numbers jumped to .320, 25, 85—and a .352 OBP. Would he have made that kind of progress if I hadn't gone down to the Dominican to work with him that winter? No way to know, of course, but I do know this: if I hadn't gone down there, and if he hadn't taken his game to a new level, I'd have felt like I cheated him and the organization, and I'd have spent the next off-season kicking my own butt. I don't like playing woulda-coulda-shoulda; I like to do my absolute very best and live with the consequences.

Robbie put on an even bigger offensive show in 2010, of course: .309, 29, 109, with a .381 OBP. (I love it all, but I *really* love that OBP.)

And you know what? Robbie Cano's only twenty-seven, and I believe he's just going to keep on getting better.

How exciting is *that*?

Mark Teixeira, among guys who make their living with a bat, was our top acquisition before the 2009 season. (C. C. Sabathia was also a pretty fair pickup, but he's not in my department.) On January 6, 2009, the Yankees announced the signing of Tex, a free agent, to what ESPN reported to be an eight-year deal worth $180 million dollars. His assignment: hit in the 3-hole and form, with Alex Rodriguez, the most potent 3–4 combo in baseball.

Seemed like a no-brainer. In 2008, Tex had blasted 33 home runs, driven in 121 runs, and batted .308 for the Braves and the Angels. That same season Alex had hit 35 homers, knocked in 103 runs, and batted .302 for us. If you were an AL pitcher, how'd you like to go to bed the night before a start knowing you were going to have face that pair four times the next day, especially with Derek Jeter and Johnny Damon hitting in front of them? Nightmare City.

But before talking about how that worked out, let me pose the question that raises a hitting coach's single biggest challenge: How do I help a player break out of a slump? That's the million-dollar question to everybody in my line of work. Or, when I come to the player I want to zero in on during this discussion, the $180,000,000 question.

That brings me to Mark Teixeira and April.

Take a look at Tex's basic power numbers in April since 2003, the year he broke in with the Rangers, through 2008, the season before he became a Yankee:

YEAR	HR	RBI
2003	2	7
2004	2	7
2005	6	14
2006	3	14
2007	2	6
2008	4	17

Now compare those numbers with what he did in September in the power department in that span, 2003–2008:

YEAR	HR	RBI
2003	6	18
2004	8	27
2005	9	37
2006	9	27
2007	7	24
2008	5	19

Let me do the math for you. In six Aprils before becoming a Yankee, Tex hit a grand total of 19 home runs and drove in 65 runs. In six Septembers over the same six seasons, Tex did a little better: 44 homers, 152 RBIs. Look at those numbers on the same line to get the full impact: 19 and 65 versus 44 and 152. Pretty astonishing, huh? And in case you were wondering, Tex's other months in the big leagues tell the same story—namely, that as the weather heats up, so does he, big-time.

You gotta believe that Mark Teixeira would like to see MLB move up Opening Day to May 15—at least.

Needless to say, I'd been studying his numbers and whatever film I could get my hands on, and I knew all about Tex's history of cruel Aprils by the time we began working together at spring training in 2009. We hit it off from the start, and we both were committed to getting rid of those *s-l-o-o-o-w* April starts that had plagued him since he came into the league.

In Tampa, we got down to business. He hit and hit and hit some more, in the cage and against live pitching in exhibition games. I spent more time with him than with any other Yankee; when he wanted a little time in the cage, my answer was always "Let's go!" By midway through spring training, Tex was swinging the bat great. By the time we broke camp, I was confident that we'd managed to fix whatever was broken. I would have bet anything that Tex was ready to come out of the gate in midseason form.

And then came another all-too-familiar Mark Teixeira April: 3 HRs and 10 RBIs, along with a .200 BA.

Not surprisingly, given that kind of start, the initial wall of cheers that greeted Tex at Yankee Stadium every time he walked up to the plate was pretty soon penetrated by quite a few boos. Yankees fans aren't know for their patience.

Three things, I thought, were getting in Tex's way.

The first was a wrist injury for which he turned to a little miracle of modern medicine that virtually every athlete I've ever known has resorted to at one time or another: a cortisone shot. Dr. Long played no part in that diagnosis or treatment. Time and meds did the trick.

The second was that he was collapsing his back side and letting his hands get away from his body. I showed him the fixes for both in the cage, where we spent a whole lot of time together that first month of the season.

The third and probably most important thing I did was help Tex not to get down on himself while in the throes of going 0-for-April. Let me tell you, that wasn't easy. Players don't have to be told when they're stinking up the joint. They do need to be reminded, sometimes over and over and over, that their smelly condition isn't permanent.

Tex's confidence ebbed at first, then came back, at least in part because he was a veteran who'd been there and done that. He'd experienced some pretty lousy Aprils, and he knew he had the talent and the guts to work through this one. I let him know that I was behind him all the way, that I knew it was just a matter of time, that we were going to stay positive, find out what wasn't working, and fix it.

Too many times I see a player start doubting himself and thinking in a negative manner when he catches a bad case of the S word. (Remember, the word *slump* isn't in my vocabulary.) Forget that shit! Stay the course! Believe in yourself! Believe in your talent and your ability to stay! Now lemme see ten more good cuts!

Baseball fans know the ending of this story. Mark Teixeira ended up leading the American League in home runs (39) and runs batted in (122) . . . he batted .292 . . . he placed second in the MVP voting . . . and he won his first World Championship ring.

April? Who remembers April?

Something in Mark Teixeira's DNA does, evidently. Proof? Take a look at the numbers he put up in April 2010: 2 HRs, 9 RBIs, .136 BA. That's right, his worst April *ever*.

Once again, I was absolutely stumped, utterly baffled. Tex and I had worked hard all spring, and we were sure, *absolutely certain,* that we weren't going to see a repeat of previous Aprils in 2010. No, this one was worse.

And then—*flash!*—it came to me: that wasn't Mark Teixeira up there flailing away helplessly for a solid month. It was his twin brother, the one who looks like a ballplayer but who can't hit a lick, the one who Tex, out of the kindness of his heart, lets spend a month in his uniform every season.

What, you have a better explanation?

Postscript: Tex reclaimed his uni after the last April showers had fallen and turned in a typical Mark Teixeira power season in 2010: 33

homers with 108 RBIs. The moral? If you buy Mark Teixeira in your Rotisserie League, don't panic over what he does in April.

He doesn't.

Who's on First?

Not Abbott. Not Costello. And not "I Don't Know."

(Gotta tell you, I could watch their old routine a million times and laugh my ass off every time.)

In major-league baseball, the answer to the question is usually, "A guy we need in the lineup for his bat but who can't do much else besides hit." In the American League, we have the DH slot to accommodate players like that as well, but in our league as well as the NL, first base is typically staffed by guys who—let's be polite—are not known primarily for their gloves.

That's certainly not true of Mark Teixeira, who won over the hearts of Yankees fans in his first year in pinstripes with 39 homers and 122 ribbies. First base? "Yeah," most Yankees fans would say, "that's where he plays when he's not DHing. So?"

But ask Mark's teammates and to a man they'll also rave about the way Tex plays first base. Jeet and Robbie Cano say that Mark saves them three throwing errors apiece per season with his great glove at first.

But I guess his skill as a first baseman isn't exactly a complete secret: in 2010, Tex won his fourth Gold Glove.

Hideki Matsui, our left fielder my first season with the Yankees before he moved on to full-time DH duty, is as streaky a hitter as I've ever seen. When he gets hot, nobody in the league can get him out. And when he's not? I could.

For Matsu—to the press he's sometimes Godzilla, to his teammates he's always Matsu—how often he's hot and how long he stays that way is all about staying on the ball away and setting his hands. When he's off, you'll see him bailing toward the first-base side of the box, which causes him to pull or roll over balls he should be driving straight. That's why, even though he's a lefty batter, facing lefty pitchers is ideal for him, because it makes him stay in there longer, which in turn makes him a better hitter.

The summer of 2009, every time an opposing manager waved in a lefty reliever to pitch against Hideki Matsui in the late innings with the game on the line, our dugout would rock: "They're doing it again, K-Long! They're doing it again!"

I'm telling you, our guys would get positively giddy.

How come, you might well ask? Fair question. After all, isn't lefty pitcher versus lefty hitter standard operating procedure in baseball, and especially in Yankee Stadium?

Yes, it is, but SOP got taken deep in 2009 when the lefty hitter in question was our DH. Matsu had a great year for us: 28, 90, .274. He put up those numbers in 325 at bats against right-handers and just 131 against lefties. Right, so you'd figure he must have really feasted off all those righties he saw to make up for doing poorly in those lefty-lefty matchups.

You'd figure wrong. Oh, he hit right-handers just fine: 15, 44, .271. But Matsu slammed 13 of his homers and plated 46 of his ribbies while batting .282 against *left-handers*—in 194 fewer at bats than he had against right-handers.

Pretty astonishing. I got out my calculator, and if Hideki had faced *only* lefties in his 456 at bats, he'd have had something like 42 homers and 160 RBIs.

An obvious question springs to mind: How come opposing teams didn't recognize that he was killing lefties and *never* bring one in to pitch against him if they could help it? It's not as if this was new news: over his six previous years in the majors (he was a twenty-eight-year-old rookie for the Yankees in 2003 after ten seasons in Japanese baseball), he'd always more than held his own against lefties. The season before (2008), Matsu hit .315 against left-handers, "only" .284 against right-handers. To me, there's only one explanation why so many teams kept sending in lefty relievers to face Hideki Matsui in 2009, especially in the last third of the season, when the pattern of his success against lefties was well established:

Somebody wasn't doing his homework.

Brett Gardner is a true gamer. Talk about tough! This guy comes to play *every* day. Gardy stands five-foot-ten and weighs about 185 pounds, and he can flat out fly. He has a knack for scoring runs and putting pressure on the opposing team with his speed on the bases. He adds a speed dimension the Yankees haven't had in a long while.

I remember seeing Brett when he first came up in 2008 and thinking to myself, *We've got some work to do with his swing, but the kid can play.* Guys just getting to the big leagues, my MO is to just kinda watch and let them go. They worked their butts off to get to the big leagues, and even if I see something I'd like to change, I don't want to tell them their swing won't work, and that they need to do this or that. So I just watch and mentally take notes on what I think they need to do.

The book on Gardy when he came up in mid-season 2008: no power, .250 hitter, lot of speed, good D. Textbook description for a part-timer you use as a defensive replacement, pinch runner, and occasional starter when somebody needs a rest. That was the role he filled for us in 2009, when he hit .270 in 108 games and stole 23 bases.

Gardy and I worked hard together and made a big change to his swing. We took away his stride to eliminate forward movement and put him in a better position to react to the baseball. The stride caused Brett to be late getting into the hitting position, and he had to fight to make good decisions on whether to swing or take pitches. My theory was that by getting rid of the stride he'd be able to see the ball longer and make better decisions.

We were gaining on it, but there was still one major flaw to over-come. Gardy was a slap hitter for most of his career, and in my view, he didn't use his lower half or back side properly while swinging the bat. So our next big swing project in his drill work was to focus on getting his back side into the game.

I also wanted to see him be more aggressive at the plate. He was taking too many good pitches. I wanted him to attack the strike zone and swing the bat much more than he was doing. In the big leagues, you have to attack the strike zone; otherwise, a smart pitcher will have you sitting 0–2 before you can blink an eye.

That's a bit of a catch-22 deal for Gardy, because his biggest value to the club comes from getting on base and scoring runs. To do that, to get a lot of walks, a guy's got to be willing to see a lot of pitches and work deep into the count, and nobody does that better than Brett Gardner. He has one of the best eyes in baseball; he swings at strikes and knows when a ball is just off the plate. Gardy sees as many pitches per at bat as anybody in the major leagues, and that's supervaluable to getting a starting pitcher out of the game. I sure don't want Gardy to open up his strike zone and start swinging at balls, and I don't think that's going to happen. But I do want Gardy to stay aggressive at the plate in RBI situations, even if it sometimes means swinging at a strike that's not quite "his" pitch. As I said, a catch-22 deal.

Big, big payoff. As a part-time starter, Brett played an important role in our 2009 championship run. Then in 2010, with Melky Cabrera gone to Atlanta in a trade and Nick Johnson hurt, Gardy got a shot at starting in left field, and he grabbed it, putting up a .277 BA along with a .383 OBP (eighth in the AL) while stealing a whopping 47 bases (third).

Take special note of that OBP. To me that's pretty good evidence that Gardy listens to his teacher and does his homework.

Too bad baseball doesn't have a stat for toughness. Let me tell you, I guarantee Gardy would lead the league. Here's just one example of that toughness. Before a game against the Royals in mid-July 2010, Brett got a piece of food stuck in his throat: no big deal, he figured; it'll dislodge or dissolve in a while. During the game I saw him throwing up in the john next to the dugout, and I asked him if he was okay. "Yeah, no problem," he said. "Just something caught in my throat, and I can't get water down." The thermometer hit 95 degrees that day, and getting dehydrated was a serious threat. Well, in the sixth inning, the game was called while a thunderstorm blew through. Gardy still couldn't dislodge the piece of food, so he took advantage of the rain delay to go back to the training room for a couple of IV bags of fluids. Instead of taking himself out of the game, though, Gardy came back after the tarps came off and a little later picked up a huge hit and an RBI for us. By the time the game ended and Gardy got himself to the nearest hospital, it was too late to see a specialist; the ER people said they were just going to hold him overnight for observation until the next morning. "Naaah," Gardy told them. "The pain's not bad. I'm going home. I'll check in with you guys tomorrow."

Did I mention that Brett Gardner is tough?

Well, sometimes the guy's *crazy* tough.

Jorge Posada has been a New York Yankee since his major-league debut in 1995, when he caught one inning (but had no plate appearances) as a defensive replacement after being called up in September. A five-time All-Star, he also has five Silver Slugger awards, which go to the best hitters by position each year. More important, he owns five World Series rings. For at least the last ten years, he's been one of the club's emotional leaders while playing the most demanding position on the field. To have the same guy behind the plate for all those years is a huge boost for a pitching staff; Sado knows the other hitters in the AL better than any other catcher in the league.

Ask any Yankee about Jorge Posada, and you'll get nothing but raves. Talk about passion and wanting to win! Jorge really gets after it. He's always screaming something at somebody or someone, always encouragement if it's one of our guys, something else if an opposing pitcher throws one too close to one of his teammates or an umpire blows a call. Once early in the 2010 season, when bullpen coach Mike Harkey put in a rare dugout appearance to fill in as pitching coach for the day, Sado was in top form, and Mike asked me about the third inning, "Is Jorge always like this?" I don't remember exactly what triggered the question, but I just nodded, Yep, he is. Look up the definition of intensity in the dictionary and you'll see a picture of Jorge Rafael Posada of Santurce, Puerto Rico.

He's in the last year (2011) of his contract, and he turns forty in August, so of course there's a chance that Sado will retire after the 2011 season. I hope he doesn't, but if he does, I hope he stays in the game—with us—in some capacity. The man's a true inspiration to us all, and to younger players in particular.

Sado and I have a great personal relationship, and we work really well together. It's been very rare for Jorge to struggle at the plate, but as I've said throughout the book, at times every hitter struggles. Sado is a tee guy, so when he hits a rough patch and wants to work on getting his stroke back, he comes into my office and heads straight to the tee. He's a switch-hitter, but he restricts his tee drill to batting lefty. He starts the drill working away, then high and away, and then inside, and he always finishes with ten line drives up the middle. From the right side, he does front flips, and because Sado is set in his ways—hey, he's been in the big leagues a lot of years; he's got a right—he'll only do it off someone who flips right-handed. I flip left-handed, so that means Rob Thomson has to come in from the bullpen to take over from me.

Sado made a *huge* contribution to our 2009 championship season. As I mentioned, he was coming back from a career-threatening shoulder injury that had limited him to 51 games in 2008. Was he done? That was a fair question going into 2009, and this is the way he answered it: 22 homers, 81 RBIs, and a .285 BA in 111 games. Done? I don't think so.

(Sado even stole a base! In retrospect, we should have stopped the game and awarded him the bag.)

The toughest part about working with catchers is monitoring their workload. It's a grueling position that takes a lot out of your legs, and a good swing begins with the legs, so we have to be smart about how many swings Jorge takes. In 2009, Jorge had just 438 plate appearances for us in 111 games. (This from a guy who'd *averaged* 574 PAs between 2000 and 2007.) In 2010, the number was 451 in 120 games. Fortunately for us all, Sado's been doing this long enough to understand his own swing inside out, and he's the first to know when it needs a little tweaking—or a little rest.

Sado is another set of eyes for me in the dugout. Honestly, I believe he follows our hitters as closely as I do. (Well, almost.) He's really good at seeing when somebody starts doing something out of the ordinary; he'll come over to me and say something like, "K-Long, his hands aren't loading."

Thanks, Coach Sado.

Derek Jeter believes in swinging at the first good pitch he sees. He always sits dead red, and his operating theory is never to let a good pitch go by. That approach is born out in his career numbers: 35 percent of the time in his sixteen years as a Yankee D.J.'s swung at the first pitch, compared with a major-league average of 29 percent. And it's worked: lifetime .317, over .300 in eleven of fifteen full seasons, never below .292 in that span.

So everybody should swing at the first good pitch they see, right? Yeah, if everybody was as good a hitter as Derek Jeter. As that's not exactly the case, a team needs to have three or four guys willing to pass up a good pitch, maybe two, so they can work deep into the count and maybe draw a walk. It's a risk: the third strike a pitcher throws may be a lot harder to handle than the two you let go by. But you need bodies on bases to score runs, so you need guys with the balls to wait for balls.

Jeet has the perfect day-in day-out attitude in a game where a guy who fails 70 percent of the time is considered a huge success. He's always positive and confident: he's never moody or down on himself. Has he gone 15-for-23 or 4-for-23 for the week? Can't tell by his demeanor. Derek doesn't scatter his thoughts; he's always steady, always focused. Young players tend to be emotional yo-yos. It takes a while for them to learn what an energy drain that is, to learn the value of a consistent, balanced approach. I don't know how many times I've told a young player, "Keep your eye on number 2."

Just after the All-Star break in 2010, Jeet was hitting "only" .271. Perfectly okay for most major leaguers, and especially the handful with consistent 20-HR power, like D.J. But not so okay for a guy with a lifetime .316 BA who was coming off a .334 season in 2009. In fact, .271 was the lowest Derek had been at that time of the season in his entire fourteen-plus years in the majors. (He finished at .270.)

Before home games, our players usually meet with reporters and answer questions. It can be a pain, and most players would rather be back in the clubhouse shooting the breeze with their teammates, but it's part of the deal, and they do it. Well, in mid-July 2010, a guy with a mike in his hand and a webcam held by a colleague pointing over his shoulder cornered Jeet and went, "So, Derek, can you talk a little about the slump you're in?"

Silence.

Icy stare.

To Derek's credit—and he's the best I've ever seen at handling the media—he just said, "I don't like to sit around talking about a slump," and turned to signal to another reporter to fire away.

Also to Derek's credit, he did elaborate on the subject a bit after the game to a reporter from the *New York Times*: "You play long enough, you realize there are going to be some times you don't get the results you want."

So true! So true! I wasn't there, but if I had been, I'd have been hard-pressed not to add my own two cents' worth—or more. I mean, a guy can hit the ball on the nose twenty straight at bats and not have but three base hits to show for it. Yes, Jeet had just turned thirty-six, and he was hitting fifty points below his lifetime average, so I guess the press was pursuing a legitimate line of inquiry. *But guys, this is the nature of our game! "Sometimes you don't get the results you want."*

"I'm finding new ways to get out," Jeet went on, referring to an unassisted putout by Rays 2B Reid Brignac that night on a hard grounder that didn't quite find the hole between first and second. (C'mon, how many times in a season do you see an unassisted putout by a *second baseman?*) "I just try to stay even keel, regardless. Sure, you get frustrated by the results. Fortunately, it's a lot easier to handle something like this when you're winning."

But you and Jeter worked on *something*, didn't you?

Yes, we watched some video together.

Yes, I watched as Derek spent some extra time hitting off the tee.

Yes, we did a quick run-through of the routine drill that Derek had been following since I was a player in the KC organization.

And yes, we watched some more video.

We identified a couple of minor mechanical issues, quickly addressed them, and moved on. Derek's always been the kind of guy who listens to what I have to say and makes adjustments that we both agree are needed. This game can humble you, but if you dig down deep, you can find ways to get the most out of your talent. I can tell you from personal experience that Derek Jeter *will* find a way to get it done. And there certainly is *no* problem whatsoever with the Captain's mental approach.

The second half of the season kicked off and we were still waiting for Jeet to get hot. Anyone who knows Derek Jeter knows it's just a matter of time until he catches fire and goes on one of his red-hot streaks. But in mid-August, Jeet's BA was down to .260. There was concern throughout Yankeeland, and rightfully so.

In the second week of August, D.J. and I got together before a game in Texas to examine the situation and identify what needed to be done. As always, he was great, but both of us knew we needed him to get his swing right in order for us to have a chance at winning our twenty-eighth championship. With Jeet, the first priority is always the same: *winning!*

In all my years in the game, I've never seen another hitter able to do all the things at the plate that Derek Jeter can do. He's the best in the business at staying inside the baseball, and hitting balls to the opposite field. He can pull it when he wants to. He can work a count. He can hit for power. He can hit for average (over .300 eleven of the previous fifteen seasons going into 2010). Unfortunately, we just weren't getting the results we both wanted. We needed to find his swing.

I had a couple of thoughts about how to fix his hitting woes, one of which I could help him with and another that was out of my hands.

My diagnosis was that Derek's stride foot was causing most of our headaches. He was gaining too much length with his stride foot and crossing over with it. Crossing over means he was striding toward the plate, a move that blocks your body off and causes the swing to get long. I'm a big proponent of working in line and being direct or square to the baseball, and D.J. wasn't there.

So we headed for the cage. We worked off the tee. We did front flips. And finally I threw him some extra BP. We agreed that his main focus was to be on keeping his stride foot down and in place throughout his whole swing. We both felt this would help both his stride length and direction. I thought his work was great, and we were both satisfied with what we accomplished. Jeet admitted it didn't feel great yet, but that he was willing to do the best he could with it and take it to the plate.

The bottom line? The next thirteen games starting September 12, Jeet got a hit in every game. He finished the season getting a hit eighteen of his last nineteen games.

Shorter stride. Straight, not toward the plate. Square. For the rest of the season, Jeet employed that formula most of the time, hit over .300, and boosted his final average to .270. Low for Derek Jeter, to be sure, but holding promise for 2011.

The other factor hobbling Derek through the first two-thirds of the season? In my opinion it was the fact that Derek's contract was set to expire at the end of the year. D.J. had been the face of the franchise for sixteen years. He had five World Championship rings. He was the team captain. And he had always conducted himself in utmost professional style—on and off the field. All that, and yet his status for the 2011 season, when he would turn thirty-seven, was unclear. I never heard Jeet say a single word about the matter, and what might happen, but I sensed it was wearing on him. Maybe I'm dead wrong, but not knowing your future can be a little nerve-racking.

Needless to say, I'm thrilled that in early December, Jeet and the Yankees agreed to a new three-year contract. Yankee for life? Hey, I don't own a crystal ball, but know I can't even imagine Derek Jeter wearing anything but pinstripes.

Now Coming to the Plate, Marcey Long

During the regular season, when I'm in New York, I usually make it out to the Stadium for one game every home stand.

But the playoffs? A totally different story. I wouldn't miss a single playoff game, home or on the road. In 2009, for example, I packed two suitcases, left Jaron (in his senior year in high school) with our daughter, Britney, and her husband, Mark (an all-star son-in-law), and flew off to NYC to help us win a World Championship. Sure enough, one month later . . . let the corks pop and the champagne flow!

On the return trip to Scottsdale, of course, my clothes no longer fit in the two suitcases I started with. What celebration doesn't include a little shopping?

Before the first game of the AL Division Series against Minnesota, Kim Girardi gave all the wives and girlfriends charm necklaces. When a game got tough, we would blow on the charms and hold them in our hands. (Our little ritual worked right out of the box: we swept the Twins!)

We all wore matching navy blue scarves. They became part of our uniform and made us feel like a team. Plus, on those chilly October nights in the Stadium, they kept us warm and cozy. (They also helped us beat the Angels 4 games to 2 in the AL Championship Series.)

We had a theme song: "I Got a Feeling," by the Black Eyed Peas. We'd text the lyrics to each other before games. We'd sing it in the stands when the Yankees would come to bat trailing in a tight game.

Don't know it? This is the way it begins:

> *I gotta feeling that tonight's gonna be a good night . . .*
> *that tonight's gonna be a good night . . .*
> *that tonight's gonna be a good, good night!*

Catchy, huh?

And anytime I want to, I can listen to Mick and Renée Kelleher singing it to me in a happy, loud version they left on my cell phone on November 5, 2009, the day after we beat the Phillies in Game 6 of the World Series to win the World Championship!

Trust me, that's one voice message I am never going to erase.

The title "World Champions" has a nice ring to it—and a really terrific *ring* that comes with it.

By the end of spring training—but not until the very end, I promise; I was seriously caught up in my work—I was counting the hours until 1:05 Tuesday, April 13, 2010, our home opener against the Angels. As I conducted the countdown in my head I was like, "Please, Lord, don't let there be a rainout! No rainout! Please!"

Well, it was 55 degrees under cloudy skies up in the Bronx, but there wasn't a drop of rain. We beat Anaheim 7–5 to bring us to 5–2 on the young season. Andy Pettitte pitched 6 strong innings (5 hits, no runs, 6 Ks) to get the W, with Mo notching his third S while bringing his ERA all the way up to 0.00. Jeet, Alex, Robbie, Sado, and Grandy went a collective 13-for-24 with 6 RBIs. Nick Johnson knocked in the other run with a homer.

I'd call that a Long day, wouldn't you?

But the high point of the day for me came before the game even started when the PA system boomed out "Hitting Coach, Kevin Long."

I practically sprinted to the podium set up on the infield grass in front of home plate where Joe Girardi, flanked by Whitey Ford and Yogi Berra, gave me a little box. My heart was beating so fast I thought I might explode. I opened the box and there it was, my ring. I slipped that beautiful baby on as fast as I could. Man, just thinking about it now gives me goose bumps.

As soon it was safely on the second finger of my right hand, I looked up at the family section just above the dugout on the first-base side and spotted Marcey and Jaron. She told me later she was crying. (Jaron just wanted to try the ring on.) All I could think of was how far we'd come together—and how happy I was that our journey was still far from over.

My long-range goal in baseball? To run out of fingers and thumbs.

GRACIAS, ENTRENADOR

BY ROBINSON CANO

Midseason 2004 I was promoted to Triple-A ball in Columbus. My first day there, I worked with Kevin Long. He had me hit some balls off the tee while he watched. And watched. And watched some more. Then we went to side toss and it was the same thing. He watched, but didn't say much besides "Good cut!" and "Way to follow through!" and "Sweet!"

Swing! "Good cut!"

Swing! "Way to follow through!"

Swing! "Sweet!"

This went on for our first three or four sessions.

During games my first week there, it was more of the same, always positive, always encouraging. Hit a hard liner right at somebody? "You hammered it!" Strike out swinging? "Tough pitch, you'll get him next time!"

Fine.

Great.

I mean, all players like to hear words of support from coaches and managers and teammates. You pop up, you don't want your hitting coach looking the other way when you come back to the bench. You take some extra swings off the tee, you want him to see how much you're sweating.

But I couldn't help thinking, *When's this guy going to give some tips I can use? Is he a coach or what?* See, I was twenty-one at the time, and like a lot of twenty-one-year-olds, I was a little . . . cocky. The Yankees had signed me as a free agent when I was eighteen, and they'd fast-tracked me through their minor-league system. I'd just been promoted to Triple-A, the take-off point for the majors. I'd been playing baseball since I could walk in my hometown of San Pedro de Macorís, in the Dominican Republic. I figured I knew everything about hitting a baseball.

Then one day Kevin said, "I know you can hit, but you've got to stop helping out the pitcher."

Say *what?* He's saying I'm *helping* the pitcher? I was hitting .301 when the Yankees moved me up from Double-A at Trenton in the Eastern League to Columbus. And this guy's trying to tell me I'm *helping the pitcher?* Man, I'm *killing* the pitcher.

I was getting ready to say all that out loud when he went on . . .

"You need to be more patient up there," he said. "You're swinging at strikes, usually, but you're not waiting for *your* pitch. Too often—not all the time, but too often—you're swinging at *his* pitch. Be patient. Wait for *your* pitch."

We talked about a lot of other stuff those last couple of months of the 2004 season in Columbus, mostly technical tweaks like turning my shoulders slightly. But one of the most important messages I took with me into Yankee Stadium when the Yankees brought me up in May 2005 was those six words from Kevin nine months earlier.

Be patient. Wait for your pitch.

I didn't follow that advice all the time—okay, I didn't follow that advice a lot of the time. But my first three years in the majors, I put up some good numbers. In 2005, I came in second in the AL Rookie of the Year voting to A's reliever Huston Street. The following season, I hit .342—my best in the majors so far—and I was a player pick for the All-Star team, but I couldn't play because of a strained hamstring that cost me six weeks of the season. (Three of my teammates represented us well: Derek, Alex, and Mariano.) In 2007, Kevin's first year as Yankees hitting coach, I had another good year: 19 homers and 97 ribbies, with a .306 BA.

Seeing Kevin get promoted before the 2007 season was great. I liked the guy back in Columbus. He was always so enthusiastic, so positive, always ready to help all the guys. But hey, I'd put together three strong years in the big leagues, and while I would work with Kevin some, mostly hitting off the tee and side toss, I have to admit I was thinking, *I'm going good, I don't need any extra work on my hitting.*

Then 2008 happened. Talk about bringing a guy down to earth! I fell off all across the board: I hit just 14 homers and batted only .271— *thirty-five* points below the season before. Even more disappointing, I scored only 72 runs, down from 93 in 2007. Isn't scoring runs the name of the game? We came in third in the AL East, out of the playoffs for the first time in fourteen years, and I felt like I'd been a major contributor to that lousy finish.

"Robbie, this is Kevin. How they hangin', my man?"

The call came in November, just before Thanksgiving back in the States. I was home in San Pedro, playing some winter ball, having good times with my family.

We talked about this and that, ballplayer bullshit, and then Kevin came to the point of the call: "How about I come down to San Pedro for a little visit after the holidays? I'd like to work with you on a few things."

My reaction? Honored. I knew that even before he'd put on a Yankees uni for the first time, he'd gone to Florida before spring training to work with Alex.

"Hey, man, that would be great," I told him. "I'd love it. Let me check with my family, and I'll get back to you on a date. You'll love it here! It's beautiful!"

Anyway, Kev broke up his own winter vacation in Arizona to come see me in San Pedro in January 2009. He describes the kind of things we worked on in Chapter 14, so I'm not going to go back over them here. But I do want to say that the visit was a perfect measure of the man: full of his dedication, his enthusiasm, and his love of his work.

The strongest thing about my man, Kevin Long? His eyes. More than any other coach I've ever worked with, at any level, Kevin can look at a guy's swing, see all its parts, see how they're working together, see what's *not* working, and come up with a plan for making it better. Other guys I've talked to, they say the same thing. K.L., he's got X-ray eyes, I swear.

And the payoff of that visit and of all the work that he and I have done since then over the past two seasons? Well, you can look up the numbers, but let me tell you the one that K-Long is proudest of: .381, my on-base percentage in 2010, the best in my six years as a Yankee.

Be patient.

Wait for your pitch.

¡Gracias, Entrenador!